T0303511

SHOT

SHOT

A Rifle's True Tales of a Prairie Farm

Willard Jackson

ELM HILL

A Division of
HarperCollins Christian Publishing

www.elmhillbooks.com

Shot
A Rifle's True Tales of a Prairie Farm

Published in Nashville, Tennessee, by Elm Hill, an imprint of Thomas Nelson. Elm Hill and Thomas Nelson are registered trademarks of HarperCollins Christian Publishing, Inc.

Elm Hill titles may be purchased in bulk for educational, business, fund-raising, or sales promotional use. For information, please e-mail SpecialMarkets@ThomasNelson.com.

Library of Congress Cataloging-in-Publication Data

Library Congress Control Number: 2018953410

ISBN 978-1-595558916 (Paperback)
ISBN 978-1-595558930 (Hardbound)
ISBN 978-1-595558923 (eBook)

THIS BOOK IS DEDICATED TO:

Rudy, of course.
Upon reading the book, you'll see why.

CONTENTS

Introduction

Farm life somehow turns farmers into storytellers—not story fabricators. Because their actual experiences are genuinely remarkable, farmers rarely contrive their stories. They can speak forthrightly because, as the saying goes, "truth is often stranger than fiction." Embellishment, though rarely a temptation, would render an account beyond anyone's reach.

Every farm has unique and sensational moments. They come to life with the farmer's rumination. While plowing the North Forty, or "driving" cows down the lane, or waiting out a long winter, farmers have time to reflect and recognize the intrigue of their seemingly routine work. They ponder the distinct circumstances and form the prose that enlivens their accounts.

Perhaps the routine of a farm redeems the significance of these events. They stand out and bear repeating if the repetition is efficient and entertaining while being accurate. Accuracy to farmers is akin to truth. "Telling it like it was" is part of their unwritten code. That does not mean they relate every detail—the day's temperature, the height of the sun, the weight of the wife, the soil accenting one's coveralls, or the surly demeanor of the family pet. No, a farmer sorts out these details and bears down on those that bring out pertinent facts.

For sure, some farms generate more stories than others. The more diversified the farm products, the more stories. The more varied the machinery, the more stories. The more differentiated the employees, the more stories. And so it goes: more seasons, types of animals, years of operation, land types, vehicles, and family members equal more stories. All of these, and many beyond them, characterized the farm life you are about to experience. Thus, stories abound for this farm, and from them you get the best of the best— as they say on the farm, the cream of the crop.

Farm accounts flow like narrative biographies in that they take certain liberties to keep them interesting—again, to repeat—while being authentic. For example, conversations approximate what was said and may be condensed from more than one occurrence. In fact, some conversations may have involved interjections by persons who are omitted in the story. To share such superfluous detail would derail or bore any otherwise interested souls. You are spared that abuse.

One more thing, a good farm story requires a good storyteller. You're going to love Shot. Prepare to meet him in the first paragraph.

CHAPTER ONE

RUDY'S FARM

Hi. I'm Shot.

More than my name, shot is my condition: worn, rusted, and broken in two. I have been around a long time, and I've gone through a lot of "situations." Through them all, I've seen things that dig at others' character and my own identity.

What I was, and still am, though disabled, is a Model 67 Winchester .22 caliber long-barrel rimfire rifle, a bolt-action single-shot equipped with a wing-style safety. With a rear, adjustable sight, I was crafted in the day of marksmanship—one shot was all that was needed.

Of course, a single shot requires a marksman. Mine was Rudy, a farmer on the North Dakota prairie. His farm was a mosaic operation—corn, grain, sheep, dogs, cats, hogs, chickens, horses, and a small dairy, complete with cows, calves, steers, and bulls. One could write a book about the latter and call it *Bull Stories*. You wouldn't put it down. I know, because I lived through a few. I'll tell you a couple.

That kind of farm is labor-intensive, and you will probably not be surprised when I tell you that Rudy had a stream of hired hands to help. Among them was a steady man who lived on the farmstead in a one-bedroom, coal-fired house. (It also had running water, if someone ran to get it, and for a toilet, picture an outhouse—a three-seater!) As the on-site employee, the hired man worked the full range of farm issues and was usually trustworthy, loyal, and dedicated to being a faithful farmer himself—a right-hand man. Although he would move on in time, typically he stayed for several years, living on the farm with his wife and sometimes one or two kids. The work would not make them well-to-do, but the farm was home because Rudy provided housing, electricity, coal, fair pay, and a feeling of partnership. The hired man was valued, and he felt it.

Rudy had that effect on a lot of folks. He liked people even when they weren't so likable. Maybe that's what serving in the U.S. Army during World War II does to a person. Although Rudy never saw action on a foreign field, he served his country during the war doing whatever he was assigned. Mostly that was logistics labor. In other words, he loaded and unloaded supplies for the fighting forces; for this he was paid little, but also, for this he paid the price of his left leg.

After unloading a flatbed railcar, Rudy and his buddies—everyone was so qualified for Rudy—sat on the end of the car hanging their legs in the gap before the dock, to eat their rations. What began as a luncheon repose became pandemonium and tragedy when an oncoming train was not switched properly onto its own sidetrack. Rudy's leg was crushed below the knee.

Amputation was required. With months of recuperation, physical therapy, and training with an artificial limb, Rudy was on "his feet" again, albeit one leg was what he thereafter referred to as "wooden." It was actually plastic, molded for fit and some flexibility as well as appearance, allowing Rudy to wear pairs of matching shoes or work boots. Only when a discussion forced the subject did Rudy comment on his leg. And with only a slight catch in his gait, many people did not realize his disability. Still, his mobility was limited.

I think that's why he was such a sure shot: in his life, on the farm, and with people, he stayed calm, aimed straight, and calculated efficient and effective actions.

When the war ended in the late 40s, Rudy returned to North Dakota to live the life so many fellow soldiers were denied because they, unfortunately, had paid the price of not just limb, but life itself. He chose to live near his family, and with consolation money from the train company, he bought the farm adjacent to his father's. It lacked fertile soil, but it was near home and those he knew. Because much of the land was not prime for raising crops, he diversified to make a go of it. Consequently, life on Rudy's farm was dynamic, replete with adventures and, of course, ripe for stories.

Before I launch into them, you should get acquainted

with Rudy's family. I knew the oldest as Tommy. That's what Rudy called him. He even called him that after Tommy became Tom and later Thomas. Tommy had a younger sister and two considerably younger brothers. I just saw them as the Little Brothers. They grew, of course, but compared to Tommy, I always thought of them as little. You know, younger means little.

Everyone contributed, especially Mother who managed the chicken and egg production and who faithfully prepared amazing around-the-table farm meals to keep everybody running strong. And usually, they were prepared from scratch, as in growing and harvesting a garden, raising and butchering chickens, and preparing and processing butter. Although after a few years, the latter gave way to being store-bought.

All the members of the family were relatively tall and lean, except for Rudy. He inherited genes that somehow were not passed on. To his chagrin, he was usually overweight and, though of medium height, he had a round appearance. Once he played Santa Claus, but only once—being typecast did not suit his fancy.

Rudy's family valued God and prayer. Good thing, too, because at times divine intervention was all that seemed to keep things afloat. There were years of drought, years of diseased animals, and years of grasshopper infestations, hail, or crop blight. And some years brought two or more of these devastations. In addition, tragedy struck more than once. Knowing God and His grace was a source of strength and seeking to glorify Him provided purpose.

North Dakota is not redneck country. The people are composed and proudly American, yet when I knew them—in the 50s and 60s—they seemed acutely aware of each other's country of origin. To hear them reference one another, you'd think that they all came from the land of stubborn. We had stubborn Swedes, stubborn Norwegians, stubborn Dutch, stubborn Germans, stubborn Czechs, stubborn Poles, and stubborn Irish. (Come to think of it, I knew someone with a French name. I'll bet he was stubborn, too.)

If they were indeed stubborn, it was probably an outgrowth of determination, the kind that propels folks to leave their kin and country, cross an entire ocean, and traverse half a continent to happily accept a government-provided quarter section of land,[1] plow its virgin soil, and make a life for a family, even when winters last forever, often at temperatures below −20°F. These were homestead roots,[2] and they sprouted dogged fruit that could at once be fiercely independent and genuinely communal. Together they built the American dream, latticing the land with roads, electrical lines, and telephone wires. They valued enterprise and education, and they, for the most part, evidenced their American pride by speaking proper English.

Of course being unique, each person had distinctive expressions. Rudy's was "Had better," as in "Had better

---

[1] A quarter of one section of land is 160 acres. That was the size of land the government gave to persons willing to break ground and farm the prairie.

[2] Homesteads were the farms established on the quarters of land. See above. Often homesteaders crafted sod houses from the virgin ground they plowed. They were hearty people.

plow the South Forty," "Had better fix the swather,"[3] "Had better cut[4] those calves before it gets hot." (Yes, in spite of the long winters, summers in North Dakota could be hot, very hot, and sometimes humid.)

Before I share some goings-on, I have one final perspective: on Rudy's farm, I was a tool. I had jobs to do. Everybody and everything on the farm was a tool in this sense: you had to earn your keep. We never fought this reality. Instead, we embraced it and took honor from it. Being a slacker, cutting corners, or causing trouble was out of the question, and if one did stray—man, beast, or machine—one was gone, or rebuilt...as you will see.

---

[3]   A swather is a farm implement that cuts hay or grain crops and forms the cuttings into a row, called a windrow. A swather is also called a windrower.

[4]   To cut a calf is to castrate it, removing its testicles.

CHAPTER TWO

CHUB

A good farm dog is worth its weight in gold. Besides being a playmate and a companion like a city dog, a farm dog works to make the farm work. He or she—gender does not matter—barks to alarm others of visitors or intruders, chases cattle to hustle them along, herds sheep, rids the farmstead of varmints,[1] and, yes, occasionally rescues family members from danger. Chub was all of that and more.

Yes, Chub. Rudy gave him that name when he brought him home as a pup. It seems he found Chub at some farm sale[2] many miles away. He was a collie, well, mostly. Raised under Rudy's supervision he came to love farm life. Without a whimper, he slept in the outdoor doghouse during bru-

---

[1] Varmints are troublesome wild animals, usually of small or medium size.

[2] Farm sales were often held when a farm was going out of business. Typically, a farm sale was conducted as an auction on its property. All items of value would be sold, even dogs and their litters.

tal winters with only foam insulation on the ground. In the hot summers, he would leap into a slough[3] filled with stale water, bugs, frogs, and who knows what to paddle about, refreshing himself. Although given milk to lap up each morning and prepared dog food to eat, Chub preferred to hunt for his food. He was good at it largely due to his forte in running, and run he did, with blazing speed.

For example, when the steers[4] in the far pasture were to be rounded up, Chub eschewed riding in a vehicle. Instead, at the declaration, "Get the cows," he'd spin in circles anticipating the adventure and waiting for Rudy, Tommy, or any others to hop into the pickup. As they pulled out of the driveway, Chub commenced racing the truck for the mile and a half to the pasture's second gate. When accompanying Tommy on horseback, Chub would occasionally scare up a jackrabbit. They would all give chase until the rabbit slipped through a fence or headed into a field of grain.[5] Then Tommy would pull up, but not Chub. He'd leap over the fence or dash into the field, and, in hot pursuit, he'd soon vanish from sight. An hour later you would find Chub at the farmstead, showing off his catch...and his supper.

Chub hunted during the night, too. When Rudy emerged from the farmhouse each morning before 5:00 to commence the morning milking, Chub might be waiting at

---

[3]   Sloughs are common in North Dakota. They are low areas where water drains and stands, typically evaporating in the summer unless replenished by rainfall.

[4]   Steers are castrated male cattle.

[5]   Grain fields could be easily disturbed by large animals, such as a horse. Where the horse trod, the grain was destroyed.

the stoop proudly exhibiting his quarry. Other times Chub might be begging for a "first responder" to render aid required to recover from hunting expeditions gone awry. If he "got into" a porcupine, his face and mouth were speckled with quills. Chub would approach Rudy with whimpering eyes, so Rudy would draw his pliers—except for church, he never went anywhere without them—and pull out a quill. Chub would yelp in pain, run off, and then saunter back for another extraction. The process continued until all quills were removed.

If Chub "got into" a skunk, Rudy's response was quite the opposite. "You beggar,"[6] Rudy would say. "Get away. You stink." It then would be days before the scent subsided or Chub masked it with other odors, say of the barn or a nearby slough.

Chub also had other nighttime expeditions that did not involve hunting, well, not hunting for food. You see Chub was given to heeding the yelps of neighboring bitches in heat. Let me explain: a female dog is a bitch—city folk call them girls, and they call male dogs, boys. Well, on the farm we called things the way they were. But if it helps you understand, consider the phrase "boys will be boys." It seems that is true even among canine companions.

Actually, a female dog in heat can attract a passel of males, and you can probably picture Chub racing to the challenge. When he prevailed, only the other farmer was the wiser...when the litter arrived. If Chub were discovered in his quest, he might be shot—perhaps with a .22 much

---

[6]   Rudy would use the term *beggar* for animals that were troublesome or annoying. In this case, Chub truly was begging for help.

like myself—without anyone knowing to whom the collie belonged. Or he might be caught and canned. So it was for Chub once or twice. Then, Rudy would find Chub at the stoop, with twine wrapped tightly around his tail and tin cans trailing behind so as to frighten him into running back to his home. In fact, the cans may be missing, having snagged on trees, brush, fences, or buffalo wallows.[7]

Chub's athleticism and high testosterone were neither wasted on the cows nor the bull. Both feared him but for different reasons. The milk cows dreaded the call of, "Here, Chub!" Even more alarming was the command, "Sic 'em!" At either pronouncement the herd, even when carrying full bags of milk, would break into a run. Why? Because Chub, recognizing the call to action, would sprint to the cows, leap through the air, and catch one of their tails in his teeth. After swinging from one side to the other, he would hang on, growling and dragging behind the terrified critter. To Tommy or anyone else watching it was hilarious; to Chub it was a sport; to the cows, death would be more welcome. One could tell from their short tails which cows were generally at the rear of the herd.

The bull—called Herman by the Little Brothers—resented

---

[7] Technically, a buffalo wallow is a natural topographical depression in flat prairie land that holds water from rain or snow runoff. Buffalo in years past would drink water from them. To us on the farm, buffalo wallows were patches of irregular ground consisting of humps one to three feet high covered with native grass. They could be found near creeks where water had flowed for thousands of years. Their shapes suggested buffalo wallowing in soft soil. As a matter of practicality, buffalo wallows could only be traversed on foot or on horseback, which may be required to find a calf hidden by its mother. Buffalo wallows lay across one of Chub's paths for nighttime interludes.

Chub "messing" with his cows. Each evening during the milking, he would–square off against Chub on a short mound in the farmstead's pasture. It was never clear why that arena was chosen evening after evening, but it was there that battle was routinely waged.

Herman pawed the ground, throwing dirt over his front shoulders and his back. While doing so he bellered[8] loudly, very loudly, and Chub barked, loudly, very loudly. People two miles away complained of the tumult. Herman would charge at Chub who would sidestep the lunge and often dart to the bull's rear to bite his heals. The bull would spin and attack again. This could go on for over an hour. At times Chub would fake going one way and then slip the other way to nip an ear. He was taunting a 2,000-pound bovine bent on burying him. Chub, however, was invariably the victor.

Knowing the outcome did not deter Tommy and the Little Brothers from routinely watching. The spectacle was unfailingly comical—cheap entertainment.

Perhaps being the heroic victor in each evening's bull-fight endeared Chub to the Little Brothers. To them, Chub was the best. He was certainly good for them. In many ways, he had been their protector during their early years. When crossing the barnyard, Chub was there to escort them. No cow, hog, or rooster dared to intercept their path without Chub giving them sufficient chase to thwart any similar future inclination.

In addition, as a little guy, seeing a dog racing alongside

---

[8] A bellow is a deep hollow sound and may be considered typical of bulls. A bull in distress or combat, however, bellers, a combination of yell, holler, and bellow.

the car was exhilarating. And seeing Chub proudly display his wildlife catches made the Little Brothers imagine him with vast powers. Cementing their pride in their dog were weekly episodes of *Lassie* on television (black and white in those days). This amazing collie consistently overcame insurmountable odds to "win the day." Chub was their collie, and to them whatever Lassie could do, so could Chub.

Chub was utilitarian, enterprising, sporty, entertaining, and endearing, a real contribution to the farm. Yet he met his demise...not from a hunt gone foul, or a romantic tryst turned deadly, nor from a misstep in a bullfight. Nope. Rather, you might say chickens got him killed.

Chickens. The farm had two kinds: layers and broilers. The former was purchased and delivered as White Leghorn chicks and raised to one day produce eggs. The latter kind was usually delivered in the spring in three waves, fifty chicks each time, with three weeks separating their arrival. Each fifty came in a large box with small holes along the sides and across the top. Little fuzzy heads could be seen popping out and emitting winsome peeps. But they weren't purchased for cuddling. No, their sole purpose was providing meat for the family and farmworkers during the summer and early fall.

They were raised in their own coop[9] with its own chicken yard. After some grew to weigh a few pounds, they were ready to fulfill their role. On Monday mornings Tommy would head to the broiler yard to snare five or six chickens with a long wire chicken catcher—the wire had a hook on

---

[9] A coop is a small building that houses chickens. A large building for chickens is called a chicken house.

one end to snag a chicken's leg. He would then pull off their heads,[10] and carry them by their legs to the shop. There, Mother would pour near-boiling water in six-gallon buckets, scald the chickens, pull out their feathers, and take them to the house for butchering. By noon a couple of broilers were cut into pieces, rolled in flour, salt, and pepper, and placed into a sizzling frying pan. Fried, fresh chicken. After toiling all morning in the fields, nothing is better, especially when complemented by mashed potatoes, gravy, garden vegetables, fresh bread, and some form of pie for dessert—Tommy preferred apple, made with extra cinnamon and nutmeg.

Sorry if that description got a little long, but I had a point to make: meals are a very important part of farm life—they are necessary for sustained life, hearty labor, and around-the-table camaraderie. And meat is essential to a good farm meal. In that, chickens were a primary source.

Unfortunately, Chub took a liking to chicken meat, too, but his appetite compromised others' lifeline and pleasure. If Rudy and his family ate chicken, it was good. If Chub ate chickens, it was bad. His nightly expeditions to the chicken house could not be tolerated.

The broiler coop was reinforced with boards, double latches, and fencing. Chub's chicken pursuits were thwarted...for a while. Before long he'd steal over to the broiler yard during the day and then, leaping over or

---

[10] This is commonly called the broomstick method of killing chickens. The bird's head is placed on the ground, comb upward. Then a narrow piece of wood, such as a broom handle, is placed over the back of the neck up against the comb. One stands on either side of the stick and pulls upward, holding the chicken's legs. The neck stretches, snaps, and severs all in one motion.

crawling under the fence, he would "hunt" chickens. Rudy applied other measures to stop the intrusions, but he knew that once a dog gets the taste of chicken, it rarely mends its ways. Mother stated the obvious but harsh verdict, "That dog has to go!"

Each morning the hired man arrived at the milking parlor between 7:00 and 7:15. Rudy would normally change clothes and then head to town for breakfast, joining other farmers. It was a great time to catch up on the news, farming practices, grain prices, and gossip. One morning, however, breakfast was postponed.

At the time, I was stored in the shop, standing in the corner atop the counter. When Rudy pulled me down, I knew it was going to be all business; Rudy did not look forward to what he had to do. In my chamber, he inserted a "long" cartridge.[11] He put a couple more in his pocket, just in case. Then he whistled for Chub. "Get the cows!" Rudy called out. Chub, though confused by the early morning summons to the pasture, danced with anticipation. They were off.

––––––––––––––––

The extra cartridges were not needed.

At the noon meal, the Little Brothers asked, "Where's Chub today? We haven't seen him."

––––––––––––––––

[11] Long is one size of a cartridge for .22 caliber rifles. Cartridges are one of three sizes: short, long, and long-rifle. The longer the shell the farther the bullet carries, and the more firepower it supplies. It was generally regarded that shorts, when shot level to the ground, would travel one-half mile; longs, a mile; and long-rifles, one and one-half miles.

Rudy looked up, glanced at Mother, swallowed hard, and said quietly, "Sons, this morning I took Chub on a one-way hunting trip."

One way? In a moment, everyone absorbed Rudy's meaning, and each excused himself from dessert.

CHAPTER THREE

CHRISTMAS HAM

One year, mid-fall, after the morning chores, Rudy sized up the situation for Tommy. "Okay, we're all set. Soon we'll have that hog you call Split Ear loaded and off to the butcher. Get the Huh-ha and wait for me inside the gate of the south pasture." With that, he placed me, barrel down, into the front of the pickup truck and headed for the gate himself. We had a job to do. My part was to kill the pig.

Now, Split Ear was a barrow[1] that had been treated especially well in that he had received extra portions of grain for the last few months—and eating is something we all know pigs emphatically enjoy. But Split Ear had not always been so fortunate: when a piglet, he somehow suffered a torn ear. Perhaps he caught it in a fence or hooked it on the corner of a feed trough, or maybe his mother stepped on it while he was sleeping. In any case, his ear

---

[1]   A barrow is a male hog that was castrated before reaching sexual maturity.

17

distinguished him, making it easy to single him out…even for fattening.

The Huh-ha was an F-20 Farmall.[2] Well, that's what Rudy said it was, but originally built in the late 30s the accumulative effects of sunlight, weather, and rust eliminated any branding. Doesn't matter, because this all-purpose tractor that once made horses obsolete for farming was itself unable to measure up in the 1950s. So Rudy modified it. He retained its overall appearance, especially its tricycle design, with two front wheels narrowly spaced together. Other than that, it was significantly reconfigured. He added a front-end bucket for scooping and dumping silage, rocks, manure—whatever needed transport. During haying season, it was equipped with long teeth and a push board to build haystacks. To keep it from tipping forward when hauling heavy loads, Rudy mounted on the drawbar a huge barrel that he filled with rocks for counterbalance. Its major change was a replacement Chevy motor with a foot feed instead of a standard hand throttle. With that type of accelerator, it could quickly change speeds, making it responsive for its many tasks. Under moderate strain, the reconfigured tractor sounded out a distinctive, reverberating chug *"huh-ha-huh-ha-huh-ha."* The Little Brothers came to call it "the Huh-ha." In time, the designation became everyone's.

Tommy was especially eager to get the Huh-ha

---

[2]   The F-20 Farmall was more formally a McCormick Deering F-20 manufactured by the International Harvester Company. *Farmall* was apparently a play on words to suggest all-purpose applications.

positioned so he could see the action. After all, shooting the hog had sort of been his idea.

The year before he had been tasked with getting a pig to the butcher. It was a stag.[3] Not long before he had been a boar,[4] but he had outlasted his usefulness, in that his female offspring were planned for future litters. It was time to be gone. Although he had lost much of his testiness, the stag could still be aggressive, and the job would require two persons. Hired to help was a man named Happy—strange, but that's what everyone called him, including his family, ostensibly due to his normally pleasant disposition. But that day he would not live up to his moniker: loading that hog was a disconcerting, terrorizing event!

You should know a few things about hogs. First, fattened swine are large creatures weighing 250 to 400 pounds. Second, their center of gravity is low to the ground, giving them tremendous leverage. Third, they dislike being chased. Fourth, they resist being loaded into trucks equipped with livestock racks. It seems that they know any ride in such an enclosure is not going to end well.

Tommy and Happy herded the hogs into the corner of a pen where they could be funneled through a door into a

---

[3] A stag is a male hog that was castrated after reaching puberty.

[4] Boars are mature, uncastrated male pigs. Hormones make them aggressive and leave their meat tainted and undesirable. Meat from stags is tolerable, especially if made into sausage or cured (smoked) cuts.

Quonset barn. (Rudy called it the Quonset).[5] There a pickup truck with its stock rack was waiting. As the hogs were bunched closer by the pen's corner, they anxiously scurried from side to side, grunting and snorting. Suddenly, a large sow[6] charged Tommy, heading straight for his legs. Any charge by an animal would be fearful enough, but this was an enormous beast with all its weight at knee level. Standing one's ground meant crushing pain and being upended—in a pigpen! Disgusting. Adding to the terror, the sow charged openmouthed, crocodile-like, with teeth bared, while emitting a death-crying screech-squeal. Needless to say, Tommy jumped to one side...thankful for his life.

In their next attempt, Tommy and Happy did less chasing, and more enticing, letting the hogs discover ground oats[7] inside the barn door. With caution, they singled out the stag, and coaxed him up and into the stock rack—credit going to more ground feed. When they sprang forward to close the end gate, the stag, seeing his escape route evaporating, charged. He slammed into the end gate just as the man and boy were attempting to drop in place the securing pins. They withstood the onslaught but gave way about six

---

[5] The Quonset was shaped like the semicircular, corrugated galvanized steel Quonset huts used extensively by the United States military during World War II. Rudy's, however, was taller and made of wood and asphalt shingles.

[6] A sow is a female pig.

[7] Oats were often ground, making them soft, even powdery. The resulting consistency makes it easier for animals to absorb nutrients. Furthermore, the ground feed mixes well with skim milk for hogs, or with molasses for dairy cows. Molasses, being sweet, entices cows into the milking parlor and into eating the oats that increase milk production.

inches. Too much. In a split second, the stag thrust his snout into the breach. Screeching-squealing he rammed ahead, with his mouth open and teeth flashing. Unable to sustain purchase on the slippery metal floor of the pickup, the stag's hooves thankfully slipped, yet they spun in a frenzy trying to gain leverage. In the elevated pickup, the piercing snout, with its fierce cacophony, was inches from Tommy's face as he pushed with his shoulder and all his might. Out of both desperation and defense, Tommy, with a free hand, slugged the protruding nose. Stunned, the stag momentarily lessened its lunge; the end gate was slammed in place, and the pins dropped.

With the stock rack latched, and adrenaline diminishing, never was it so satisfying for two farmworkers to drive fifteen miles to a slaughterhouse. Enough of that pig! Enough of that task!

———————

That was last year, yet the recollection was vivid, and repeating the process was foreboding.

"No!" Tommy protested to Rudy. "Dad, do we have to? Isn't there some other way to load a pig?"

Noting the anxiety in Tommy's face, Rudy came up with an idea. "Believe so. Get the .22...and my hunting knife... and the sharpening stone."

Yes, I had a role: Why go through all the trouble of loading a live pig, when the first thing that happens on the other end is killing it? My job was to reverse the order. While

Tommy ran for the Huh-ha, and as I rode in the pickup through the gate, I became anxious…reality was setting in.

Now, as a .22 caliber I am a very light rifle and my bullets are small. A hog's brain is encased in a thick skull while its other vital organs lie inches below hide, fat, and muscle. Tommy had stated the challenge when he handed me off to Rudy. "How sure are you that this rifle will do the trick?"

"Pigs have a little soft spot in their forehead," said Rudy. "I had better not miss."

Indeed! Tommy pictured a wounded, rampaging hog—multiples of terror beyond last year. He ran to position the Huh-ha, so he could watch. A sure shot would be exciting; a miss would be, well, more than exciting. Oh boy!

With me in the pickup, Rudy drove slowly toward a straw pile where the hogs were feeding and burrowing. About thirty yards away, he stopped, stepped out, and reached for me. I actually felt his confidence. With my stock high under his arm and my barrel pointed downward, we casually strolled toward the pigs. At that point, we were a team and neither of us, unlike Tommy sitting on the Huh-ha, doubted the outcome.

The hogs noted our approach, standing and looking at us as though wondering about our purpose. Were we there to remove the straw? To chase them off? To provide some special feed? Split Ear was restless and furtively looked up at us, and down, and over to the other hogs—head always moving. We strolled closer. When Rudy pushed the bolt in place and clicked back the firing pin, Split Ear curiously took note, holding his head up and straight at us. Then he looked away. When Rudy raised me to his chin, the hog's attention was arrested. What was that long object protruding from this casual, rotund farmer?

Slit Ear never knew what hit him. Rudy called to Tommy, "Come on. Let's hang him up." Tommy stepped on the gas: "*huhhhhhhhhh*"—no "*ha*"—it was full speed ahead. Tying chains to the hind legs, they hoisted up the barrow and then backed away from the straw. With a deliberate, swift motion, Rudy slit its throat and blood quickly pooled on the ground below. Then, while waiting for the blood to drain, Rudy leaned against a tractor tire, honing an edge on his knife.

In a few minutes Rudy field-dressed the hog like an experienced hunter.[8] Then he skinned it. We were ready for transport. "Lower this hog into the back of the pickup," he commanded.

You know, loading that hog was pretty easy, far easier this year than last. And the butcher even reduced his price, not having to do the front-end, dirty work.

Here's the good part:

I was placed back in my resting place in the shop, only to wait until I could be of service in some other way, some other time. Winter soon set in: each day grew colder; snow came; then it came and stayed. With the passing of about six weeks, Rudy one day drove off in the pickup, returning an hour later with two large boxes. He parked in front of the shop just as Tommy was getting off the school bus. "Come

---

[8]   Hunters field dress animals killed for meat. It is the process of removing internal organs.

here, Son," he called. "Had better take this box to the hired man. Thought you'd like to tell him 'Merry Christmas!'"

That box was loaded with gifts—life-giving gifts—each one wrapped in white paper, taped, and labeled: hocks, ribs, roast, liver, sausage, bacon, ham. The hired man, his wife, and their little girl would jump for joy.

CHAPTER FOUR

THE LANE

Every farm should have a lane. In Christmas cards and magazines glamorizing country life, lanes are pictured as idyllic passageways between rows of trees or flowering bushes. Often included are sleighs or old cars conveying passengers, joyfully, to pastoral respite.

Rudy's farm had a lane, but it lacked storybook repose. Instead of leading to pastoral respite, it simply led to a pasture about one-third mile south of the farmstead. Oh, it had a few flowers, if it was a good year for wild prairie roses, but it was rarely picturesque. Instead, it was carved with paths for cattle, sheep, and farm vehicles. What it lacked in beauty, however, was easily made up by intriguing activity. And I can assure you that picturing that action is more engaging than viewing point-in-time photographs.

The pasture was used to graze milk cows in the evening—now, that's a pastoral scene—but it was better known for harboring wild animals. Brush in the prairie grass provided cover for dens of fox or skunk, and the watering hole at its far end attracted shorebirds and waterfowl, such as ducks, killdeer,[1] and sandpipers.[2] It also was a welcome "drinking fountain" for varmints, deer, and an occasional moose.

Now wild animals, being natural to their environment, evoke awe and wonder. They did so back in the 50s, too, but then they also competed for the land that farming communities resolved to subdue. Also committed to redeeming the land, the government had bounties on many animals, especially those for which their pelts did not already reward harvesting.

I must pause here to explain. How can it be right to harvest wild animals that are simply living out a natural life? I'm a rifle, so I suspect I'm biased, but I'm also old, and I can attest to the troubles that wild animals rendered in those days. In the open country, say in a pasture, newborn lambs and calves were vulnerable. Coyotes, as you can imagine, would take advantage of these helpless creatures. But the foxes, too, would steel away young lambs. Too often, before the ewes[3] could finish birthing twins or triplets,[4] the first-born was lost to waiting, opportunistic foxes.

Even on the farmstead, not in the open country,

---

[1] Killdeer are medium-sized shorebirds. They are noisy, with a cry that sounds like "kill deer."

[2] Sandpipers are small- to medium-sized shorebirds. They are distinguished by long bodies and legs, narrow wings, and, usually, narrow bills.

[3] Ewes are female sheep.

[4] Often ewes have multiple offspring. Twins are common; triplets are not rare.

domesticated animals could be vulnerable. Chickens were especially at peril. Skunks, raccoons, foxes, weasels, and badgers[5] would sneak onto the farmstead and pursue them. When they struck, we were fortunate if only one or two chickens were destroyed. However, the critters too frequently killed several chickens in the course of making off with just one...only to return for more mischief in a night or two.

A common danger came from holes dug by the wild animals. A gopher, small as it, can dig a hole that a cow can step into and be injured. Varmints like foxes and skunks create crippling traps for the legs of unsuspecting farm animals. Most despised for holes were badgers. They would dig several large holes in close proximity in a single night, and no ground was immune, regardless of how hard it might be. These holes were death traps. I'll illustrate.

In the pasture down the lane, Tommy was once galloping his favorite horse to the watering hole when a front hoof sunk deep into a hole. The horse stumbled—no, it crashed—to its knees, smashing its head and neck on the ground and flipping end over end.

And Tommy? He went flying, catapulted through the air, crashing to the earth himself. Luckily, he did not break an arm, or a leg, or his neck. And luckily, when he looked back, his beloved horse was walking, albeit gingerly, with all four legs intact.

I told you that on Rudy's farm I was a tool, and I told you

---

[5] Badgers are omnivorous nocturnal mammals belonging to the weasel family. They have short, wide bodies with short legs, making them especially adept at digging.

SHOT

that I did what I had to do, but I always hoped that I would never be called upon to finish off a maimed horse. They are majestic creatures that serve willingly and sacrificially. If they were to require my attention, it would be from no fault of their own. Sadly, they would lie still, whimpering in a nightmare of defeat, and I would be pressed into duty at close range. I shudder at the thought...and I am glad I never encountered this responsibility.

I was, however, called upon to help "clean up" a fox den. Early one summer morning, about 5 o'clock, when Rudy was rounding up the cows for milking, he heard yelping from some brush. He immediately recognized the cries of what could only be fox kits.[6] The following Sunday afternoon, Rudy and some friends drove their pickups down the lane to dig out the den. Mother and Tommy followed in the family car. I rode with Rudy.

With pickaxes[7] and spades, they excavated the soil near holes found amidst the brush. They dug deeper and broader following a tunnel to the den. When it was about to be breached, Elden, one of the friends, called out, "The vixen's in there.[8] Get the .22!" Well, I did what was required, or you might say, Rudy took care of things.

When the pups were pulled out, Rudy's friends took a liking to them. They were cute and playful. At least one pup

---

[6] Kits are the young offspring of foxes. They are also called cubs and pups.

[7] A pickaxe is hand tool with a steel spike attached to a handle. It is used to pierce and break up hard surfaces.

[8] A vixen is a female fox.

went back to a farm with the hopes of one day being a handsome pet. I prefer to think it all worked out.

The lane was fenced, but only with a single strand of electric wire. The wire, pulsating with electricity, commanded respect from the cattle. When moving down the lane, they carefully stayed clear of the wire, and even when the grass under it compelled consumption, they carefully stretched their necks under the wire. One could see them flinch when they raised their heads too high.

Sheep had the advantage. Their short stature allowed them to walk under the wire, and if they did contact it, usually their wool was a sufficient barrier to shock. Rudy's practice was to bring the sheep through the gate at the end of the lane whenever he rounded them up. By setting the gate with an opening of only about two feet, the sheep would be forced to go through one at a time. This they did willingly because sheep naturally follow one another, and if the lead sheep knows the route and enters the gate, the others do likewise. It was quite a scene: about 500 head of sheep, bleating and ambling along—sheep are never in a hurry—often strung out over several hundred yards, until crossing under the electric wire where they bunched up waiting for a turn to squeeze through the gate. Upon getting through many of them were inclined to jump or hop with a twist or turn to "celebrate" their gate victory, or maybe it was from the joy of being home at last. Who knows?

In passing, I will answer a question you likely have: Why only a narrow opening in the gate? Hmmm, that was a practical matter for Rudy. You see, by allowing one sheep through at a time, Rudy could count them to ensure all were present. After all, 500 sheep, or thereabouts, are a lot to keep track. He counted them by twos. When asked why not by ones, he said, "Too hard to keep up. They get to coming through pretty fast." Indeed, Tommy once tried counting by ones, and he arrived at a different total than Rudy did. It had been a challenge keeping up, but still, Tommy thought he had an accurate count. When he expressed his number, Rudy simply said, "Next time count by twos; you'll get it right." He was sure of himself, and Rudy, being the way he was, was more than likely "dead on."

The most exhilarating activity of the lane was racing horses from the pasture to the farm. This was a common, cherished sport for Tommy and his friend Johnny. Adding to the excitement, each pretended to be one of the superheroes of the day. For Tommy, he was the cowboy Roy Rogers, and like Roy, Tommy named his horse Trigger. Johnny fancied the Lone Ranger, which was perfect because Johnny rode a white horse named Silver. Well, that would've been ideal, but in reality, the white gelding (dapple gray, actually) was named Pete. Little matter, when the horses were given free reign at the start of the lane, they became charging steeds, hell-bent for leather.[9]

If it had rained in the foregoing days, mud splattered everywhere with the boys absorbing way too much for their mothers' liking. If it were dry, dust billowed up and trailed them like a furious whirlwind. Although the race was dangerous, neither superhero nor his mount chanced a second

[9] "Hell bent for leather" is a colloquial expression meaning riding saddleback with reckless determination.

thought for anything but more speed. Let there be mercy…
and, at the end of the lane, an open gate!

Once it was closed. It happened that on that day Ole
Pete had succeeded in pulling off his favorite stunt, making
the race down the lane triply treacherous—raging speed,
closed gate, and a loose saddle. Here, too, I better explain.

Typically, the boys would saddle up at the shop where I
hung out. If a grown man were around, he'd be called on to
tighten Pete's cinch.[10] With Pete, this meant kneeing him in
the ribs so he would expel air he had sucked in to blow up his
chest and belly, and then quickly pulling the cinch another
inch or two tighter. Without a man's help, both boys pulled
together to tighten the cinch. They were seldom successful.
Later Pete would relax and enjoy a comfortably loose girth.[11]

In the race down the lane, Pete's saddle began to slide
off center and down one side…with Johnny on it. He was
in no position to pull back on the reins, not that it would
have mattered much once the horses had their heads.[12]
Fortunately, Tommy and Trigger, who were in the lead, spotted the closed gate and pulled up just in time. So did Pete.
As he came to a snorting, panting halt, the saddle spun
under his belly, upside down, with Johnny still gripping the
pommel.[13] When Johnny loosened his grip, he fell the couple

---

[10] The cinch is attached to a girth band.

[11] The girth is the band that goes under a horse's belly and is attached
to a saddle by leather straps.

[12] To give a horse its head is to give it free rein, allowing it to move its
head freely and proceed under its own control. In horse racing, this
usually means running unrestrained.

[13] The pommel is the projecting front part of a saddle.

of feet to the ground. To Tommy, this was comical beyond belief. To Johnny, it wasn't funny.

Ahhh, the lane—a channel of activity. Do you get the picture?

Like I said, every farm should have one.

CHAPTER FIVE

SHOTGUNS

Okay. It's time for a bull story. Brace yourself.

This account involves two shotguns, the second of which was brought in to fire shot and slugs—shot can get a bull's attention; slugs can kill him.[1] The account also involves Tommy and his horse Trigger. Neither was hurt, but both were severely frightened, and more than once. You see, they were dealing with a bull gone mad, a bull that had to be gone!

Of course, Rudy is at the center of this episode. And as usual, the hired man plays a key role. It's his fear that leads to the second shotgun.

And how might a .22 rifle fit into this picture? Against a bull, I'd be pretty much useless. My bullets would do minor

---

[1] A shotgun is a shoulder-fired firearm primarily designed as a scattergun for hunting birds and as such shoots shot, which is an array of small, round, metal pellets. Secondarily, a shotgun can be used for big game if it fires slugs, which are solid metal projectiles.

damage at best, and at worst, an already mad bull would become stupefied with fear and rage. So, this story has little to do with me. But I knew those two shotguns and through them I had a bird's-eye view.

At the time I was stored in a closet in the farmhouse. This was the closet for Rudy's outdoor gear. It had light summer jackets, medium-weight spring and fall jackets, and heavy parkas and insulated coveralls for the frigid winters. Behind all these, I stood in a corner along with two companions: a thirty-aught-six (.30-06) rifle and a 12-gauge shotgun[2]. In some years, in the fall, Rudy used the rifle for deer hunting. When he hunted, he at times successfully bagged a deer; other times he only returned with stories of his ventures. These would involve driving down prairie roads or along fence lines, hoping to scare up a buck, which typically was all Rudy had a permit to hunt. Driving, of course, was integral to his hunting because he was not able to walk more than short distances without abusing his amputated leg.

In fact, for Rudy, driving was critical not only for hunting but also for operating the farm itself. He drove to round up cattle, he drove to search for and bring home newborn calves, he drove for tanks of water, he drove to reach farm implements, and he drove to and from the fields, even if they were near the farmstead. Yes, Rudy conducted his life

---

[2] A .30-06 rifle is so named because it shoots .30 caliber bullets, which were originally adopted by the US Army. The .30-06 can be used for hunting large game, such as deer. The gauge of a shotgun is an indication of its size. Twelve-gauge shotguns are mid-sized (16- and 20- gauges also exist) and are commonly used for hunting geese and other large game birds.

by driving, which, strangely enough, brings me to my second companion, the shotgun.

No one ever used it. Stick with me.

In the 50s, Rudy mostly drove the pickup. It was a 1950 Chevrolet half-ton. Had it not been rebuilt by Rudy, it would have been long gone. He retrofitted it with a grain box that actually tilted with the aid of a hydraulic jack, and when so needed it was outfitted with a stock rack. Rudy was known to haul home two cows at a time from a livestock auction— probably exceeding the vehicle's recommended capacity. Functional as it was, the pickup was not comfortable. To the contrary, in that pickup we bounced to our destinations. Even on a good gravel road we bounced. Off road, in the pastures and fields, the Chevy was more rodeo than transport. Rudy needed a better "ride." We all did.

At a car dealership, in the city seventy miles away, Rudy found an alternative. It was a used blue-green 1954 Ford V-6 Ranch Wagon. Imagine that: a model name matching its planned use. The station wagon road like a car but had cargo space for hauling the likes of tools, fence posts, fertilizer, and, you guessed it, newborn calves. Unfortunately, Rudy lacked the required funds to purchase his fantastic find. Wanting desperately to make a sale, the salesman asked Rudy what he had of value that he might trade. After some thought, Rudy suggested the shotgun. Though skeptical, the salesman and his manager listened to Rudy's description of a choice shotgun in mint condition. They determined that if Rudy brought in the shotgun and it proved to be as good as professed, they'd have a deal.

On Rudy's and Mother's next trip to the city, along went my companion. The transaction was completed and Rudy returned with a "new"—quite used, actually—farm vehicle. Rudy called it the Shotgun. Why not? So everybody called it that.

And everyone on the farm had applications for the Shotgun. It herded the cows for milking. It chased home stray steers—sometimes veering off the road, down a ditch, and across a plowed field. It blasted through puddles and sloughs to repair fences or just to provide sport. And it stood up to an out-of-control bull—but not without damage.

The bull in question was a Brown Swiss[3] called Herman. I think every bull on the farm was called Herman. The Little Brothers named them. We had Herman, Herman II, Herman III, and so on. Every two or three years we had a new Herman—after all, a bull's utility only lasts until his heifers are old enough to calve themselves. Can't be servicing one's own offspring. (Sorry. These events are not intended to be raw; on a farm, facts of life are plainly evident.)

Now, I get confused with all the Hermans, but the one in this story may have been the same one that sparred with Chub each evening. In any case, he had similar mannerisms in that he was aggressive and loud, meaning he bellered

---

[3]   Brown Swiss are dairy cattle originating in Switzerland. They are usually dark brown in color. Typically cows weigh 1,200 to 1,400 pounds while bulls are in the 2,000-pound range. The breed is considered to be relatively docile, but being around farming operations Brown Swiss bulls, which are normally protective of their herds, can become irritated and aggressive.

loudly in frequent fits of rage.[4] Consequently, he generated fear within the family.

One night, Tommy dreamed that the bull was upset with the farmhouse, and spurred by increasing anger he charged, barging through a bedroom window. The dream was outrageous, but it felt real. Because it troubled Tommy, he shared it during the noon meal. Rudy listened and then "interpreted" the dream. He said that around four o'clock in the morning he heard the bull rampaging in the yard. He had somehow gotten out of the pasture and was standing near the house, bellering at it...on the side where Tommy slept. Rudy said he dressed, went out, climbed into the Shotgun, and tried to chase the bull back into the pasture. He succeeded but not before Herman charged the car. The front grill and a headlamp were smashed. Sure enough, on the lawn thirty feet from his window, Tommy later found a pile of broken glass. Naturally, he then had his own reasons for having that bull gone.

Apprehension over the bull increased as Tommy and Trigger were soon to experience. And the Shotgun was again targeted.

That summer the milk cows were pastured across the road from the farmstead, where they had no water source. Each noon, right after eating, someone brought the cows home to drink and then moved them back to the pasture. Tommy typically had this responsibility, and one day, desiring to make quick order of it, he swung onto Trigger's bare back and sprinted off.

---

[4]   A bellow is a deep, hollow sound typical of bulls. A bull in distress or combat, however, bellers, a combination of yell, holler, and bellow.

Herman was focused on a cow in heat and took offense at the noonday intrusion. He charged Trigger...several times. Although Tommy lacked the stability afforded by a saddle, he relentlessly drove the cows to water, cautiously avoiding the bull.

Perhaps you remember Happy from my telling you about the Christmas ham. Anyway, he was a hired hand who Rudy occasionally acquired for special projects. At this time of year, it was haying season, and Happy was engaged for mowing.[5] He saw Tommy's plight and attempted to come to his rescue in the Shotgun. The bull disliked the motorized interruption even more than that of the horse and rider. He charged the car. Happy avoided a collision, but he was unnerved. Distraught, he drove the Shotgun back to the farmstead where he found Rudy and expressed his exasperation. (It seems that when Happy worked for Rudy, he needed a different nickname.)

Frankly, Rudy was immediately concerned: his son, his ranch wagon, and his hired hand had all been endangered, and such boldness portended future incidents that might not fare so well. He declared, "Had better teach Herman a lesson." Oh boy!

It wasn't much of a vehicle, but Rudy had also "picked up" an old 1949 Ford from a neighbor. It had been a car but the rear portion of the cabin was cut off with an acetylene torch, modifying it into a two-seater pickup. It couldn't haul much but it provided field transportation, and it handled less desirable tasks than those saved for the Shotgun.

---

[5] To mow hay is to cut it. That is the first step in haying. Thereafter, it is usually raked and then baled or stacked.

Rudy jumped into the '49 while asking Happy if he wanted to join in some payback. Without time to think and not knowing Rudy's plan—Happy's mistake—he plopped into the passenger side. Rudy roared off. Tommy saw the '49 wildly ripping through the open gate into the pasture. He didn't know what was to occur, but it was obvious that he and Trigger needed to get out of the way. They galloped to a far corner.

Rudy pushed the pedal to the metal, aiming for the bull. The bull ran. Rudy smashed into him and, spinning a donut in the grass, tore after the bull again. Smash. Again, and again, sharply turning and sliding the '49, he...well, shall I say, taught Herman a lesson. Happy, however, was not happy. Over the roaring engine Tommy could hear him cursing, not the bull, but Rudy and his driving.

He lived and so did the bull. In fact, Herman developed quite a healthy respect for vehicles—call it fear. That's for sure what it was.

Still, it was time for the bull to go. One morning, Tommy with Trigger and Rudy with the Shotgun singled out and moved Herman into a corral near the far pasture. The next task was to subdue the bull and tie him up. A trucker would later come to transport him to the sales ring.[6] How do you subdue a massive Brown Swiss bull given to rage and aggressiveness? Easy. One grabs the ring in his nose.

Okay, I'll clarify. Dairy bulls often have rings inserted in their noses when they are adolescents. Because a bull's nose is extremely sensitive, a person can subdue a bull by

---

[6] A sales ring is a location for a livestock auction.

pulling on its ring. Then with a rope attached, one can lead or tie the bull in place. Grabbing the ring, unfortunately, is easily said but not easily done. So forget the "easy."

The full-time hired man at the time was named Lenn. Compared to Rudy, he was nimble of foot. Thus, Rudy directed Lenn to enter the pen and get a hold of the ring. Lenn, sitting atop a wooden gate, objected, "What if he charges?"

Rudy, always looking to save steps, retorted, "Then you won't have to chase him down." Comforting thought, huh?

"I'm not going in there!" declared Lenn. "There's no way in—"

"All right," said Rudy, with resignation. "I'll do it myself."

The plan was doomed. When a bull charges, he tucks his nose down to leverage the top of his head. Rudy, therefore, picturing himself angling for the ring, came to another idea. He pulled some wire from the back of the Shotgun and fashioned a hook on one end. With the wire, he attempted to snare the bull's ring. Tommy and Lenn, now both sitting on the wooden gate, watched nervously.

Herman was more nervous. Upon Rudy's approach, the bull bolted—straight for the gate. Son and hired man braced for a splintering crash. But at the last split second the bull veered right and jumped. In his fear, with adrenaline apparently peaked, Herman cleared a six-foot woven wire fence with the front part of his body. And although his hind legs smashed down the wire by about fourteen inches, he was free. Mind you he was also terrified and enraged. Now what?

Rudy pursued in the Shotgun while Tommy and Trigger guided the bull along a familiar route to the farmstead—the route the milk cows often took when returning home in the evenings. Lenn did what he could do following with an "M" International.[7]

At the farmstead, Herman ran through the open gate and then between two buildings—a calf barn and a shed—to the milking barn. While this was well-known territory for Herman, it also was a trap, being a boxed enclosure. In other words, the only route to escape was the one by which he entered. Rudy, hotly pursuing, slid the Shotgun sideways between the buildings, blocking Herman's retreat. Well, almost. After he inched the Shotgun forward and up tight to the shed, a six-foot gap remained to the rear. Jumping out, Rudy yelled to Tommy, "Get your horse in here. We'll wall him in."

Tommy positioned Trigger into the breach, head to the Shotgun and tail close to the calf barn. They had a barricade. The bull was again confined. Stiffened by fear he positioned himself in a corner formed by the milking barn and a windbreak made of corrugated sheet metal. His flanks were heaving and his nose and mouth foamed. Every few seconds he swung his head from side to side, alert to trouble, and as though spooked by his own shadow, he occasionally spun left or right. Clearly, he was on "pins and needles" and, consequently, extremely dangerous, yet this was a chance to subdue him.

---

[7] An "M" International is a tractor. Rudy's had a wide front-end and was likely a Super "M" McCormick Farmall manufactured by International Harvester in the early 1950s.

Lenn finally arrived on the scene, having been delayed by the comparatively slow tractor. "Run to the chicken coop and get the catcher," Rudy commanded.

The catcher was a stiff, large-diameter steel wire. Its rigidity allowed a length of about fifteen feet, on the end of which was a crook designed to snare chicken legs. This wire was longer and more maneuverable than the one Rudy had crafted earlier. Lenn ran for it, probably not realizing that he would be the one using it to snag Herman's ring.

Well, Lenn was not going in that box with the bull. And neither was Rudy. Through holes in the corrugated windbreak, Lenn manipulated the catcher trying to hook the bull's ring. It did not work. In fact, it made matters worse. The bull, already terrified, went insane when he felt the wire bump his nose. He sprang forward, sprinting to flee the box and heading directly for Trigger...with Tommy in his saddle.

Did I mention that Rudy's family was a praying family? Yes, I did.

Rudy yelled, "Here he comes!" Could the makeshift wall possibly rebuff Herman's onslaught? No, not at his speed, which was increasing. Horse and rider were about to be bowled over, no doubt with serious injuries. But amazingly, Herman gathered himself mid-stride and leaped. He cleared Trigger's rump—halfway over Trigger and half over the space between the horse and the calf barn. Tommy was safe...by at least four inches.

The bull tore through the open gate, passed the shop and the lawn where he had smashed the headlamp, into a grove of trees, bellering all the way. Herman had a case of the D's: delirious, demented, and deranged, not to mention, dangerous.

Lenn lost it. If he was to arrest a bull, he required lethal force. Wide-eyed he ran to his house and emerged with a shotgun and several shells. Normally the shotgun was used for pheasant hunting, but now it was for Herman hunting. Some of the shells were slugs. Lenn clearly had his own D's: duress, distraught, desperate, discomfited. He was determined to defend, defeat, and destroy. The bull be damned.

Rudy, upon driving the Shotgun up to the shop and seeing Lenn standing there with weapon loaded, realized that panic prevailed—for beast and man. Further pursuit would be disastrous. Through the open car window, he demurred, "Had better let it go. Tonight, the beggar can join the cows. In a few days, we'll have a better plan."

Turning the Shotgun to the driveway, Rudy headed to the fields. Tommy began unsaddling Trigger. Lenn relaxed, unloaded his shotgun, and returned it to his house.

But things were not quiet. Herman bellered and snorted in the trees for the next hour.

CHAPTER SIX

THE FOX

According to the *Random House Historical Dictionary of American Slang*,[1] the idiom "Crazy like a fox" means "seemingly foolish, but in fact extremely cunning." That would not describe me: I only performed according to the laws of physics. I yielded punch and precision but not purpose. That came from those in whose hands I was held.

Sighting in a carefree fox trotting off to breakfast requires purpose. Yes, as you likely guessed, Rudy's purpose.

Before I share the story, allow me one question: Does a fox know when it's being sly? Or does cunning come so naturally that it's subtle and spontaneous, but not mischievous?

---

[1] *Random House Historical Dictionary of American Slang*, Volume 1, A-G. JE. Lighter, Random House, New York, 1994.

"How do you know it was a fox?" asked Tommy.

"Because I saw its tracks," replied Rudy.

"Dad, how is it that you know a fox's tracks so as to distinguish them from other animals'?"

"I just know. Must have learned as a kid."

This kind of conversation between Tommy and Rudy occurred often. Tommy was logical and fact-based. Rudy didn't disregard these, but he had a deeper, mystical awareness of things and how they worked. Rudy just knew things. Tommy, on the other hand, required rationale, principles, practices, or precedent to explain, to plan, to run a business, to...well, to do anything and everything.

Tommy continued, "So, what are we going to do about this animal that's stealing our chickens? A fox, according to you."

"I'll shoot him in the morning when he shows up."

"Hold on. What makes you think the fox, if that's what it is, comes in the morning? Aren't foxes nocturnal? They hunt at night."

"Well, guess so, but just a minute," Rudy said exasperatingly. "I swear I've seen foxes hunting in daylight, especially in the morning. Maybe they do both. Anyway, why would a fox go through the trouble of prowling around in the dark when he can walk right up in the light and get what he wants? Nope, he comes in the morning."

"So, on that flimsy basis, you're going to stake yourself out in the morning hoping to shoot a fox, that you might even miss."

"I don't plan to miss."

"I don't suppose you do. But my curiosity is piqued.

Why do you have this animal—er, fox—pegged as a 'he' and not a 'she'?"

"Yeah, I am picturing a male, come to think of it."

"Why?"

"Don't know. Maybe I figured a female fox would be with her young early in the morning."

Tommy slapped his own head. What a string of assumptions! "Okay, Dad, how do you have it 'figured' that you'll surprise this fox? It could be coming from anywhere?"

"Oh, he'll be coming down the lane."

"Now you're being cocky. We have a wheat field to the west, a barley field to the south, oats to the east, and trees to the north. He, I mean, it can emerge from anywhere."

"Maybe."

"So, why are you focused on the lane?"

"Because that's where he'll be."

"But why—why say that? How can you say that? On what basis?"

Rudy, as a patient father, generally tried to appease Tommy's need for logic. "Let's see. If I were a fox, I would avoid all that tall grain and grass and just mosey on down the lane. Easy goes, easy does."

"All right, if you were a fox. But this fox, if it is that, is not likely overweight and hopping around with a missing leg."

That hurt and Tommy instantly regretted saying it. But when it all ended, Rudy felt justified. You see, he was indeed right—on all accounts.

Rudy was naturally intuitive. Oh, he had logic, but it was deep down and often so far below the surface that he could not produce it. Yet, his "sixth sense" was reliable. Allow me to digress briefly to solidify this endearing characteristic, irritating as it was to Tommy.

———————————

In the 1940s and early 50s, farmers made hay, transported hay, and "put up" hay. Rudy came up with an idea of building a haystack hauler. He had never seen one—no one had—but he was not deterred, and he succeeded. With Rudy's invention, one only had to make and transport hay. The "up" part became obsolete.

Generally, haying had three steps: mowing grass and letting it dry, raking it and letting it dry some more, and then bucking it into haystacks.[2] You then had hay. But to use it, the hay had to be moved, usually to haylofts in barns. In "the day," wagons were loaded in the field and then pulled to the farm in front of a barn. There a grapple[3] attached by ropes to a vertical pulley[4] was lowered into the wagon where a farmhand pushed its hooks deep into the hay. A large clump was raised high and then with a horizontal pulley drawn into the loft. With a trip rope, the grapple arms were released and the hay dropped. The process was long and arduous.

Rudy's brainchild not only hauled a haystack, it loaded

———————————

[2] To buck hay is to push dried grass lying in windrows into large piles, which can then be loaded into hay wagons or combined to make a haystack.

[3] A hay grapple is a claw used to hold hay. It has arms that are sunk into loose hay and squeeze together when pulled.

[4] A pulley is a combination of multiple wheels over which ropes are looped to multiply forces, increasing leverage, such that "by hand" one can lift or pull large loads.

it from the ground in the field and unloaded it at the farm site. What's most amazing is that to construct it Rudy had no instructions to follow, no drawings, and, as mentioned, no other hauler to model. Rudy's was the first, at least in our part of the country.

Well, more than just in our parts. Upon hearing about this labor- and time-saving machine, visitors came from all around to have a look. Several came from North Dakota, some from South Dakota, and at least one from Minnesota. Shoot, we even had a couple of visitors from Canada.

Each would ask Rudy if he had a haystack hauler as had been storied. Rudy would acknowledge that he did.

"Mind if I have a look at it?"

"Nope," Rudy would reply. Then he would tell where the hauler was located. The visitor would go observe, studying the implement, admiring its apparent functionality and capacity. (Like I said, it stopped traffic. It was large, and with a ten-ton haystack aboard, it appeared to take up the entire road. Rather than risk it, drivers of most oncoming vehicles pulled over as far as possible and gawked as Rudy drove by.)

When the visitor reappeared to talk with Rudy, Tommy and the hired man found an excuse to move closer, because they knew what was coming, and it never failed to make them laugh—though not in front of the visitor. The conversation, usually at the shop where I was stored, went something like this:

"Quite a machine you built."

"Yep. Saves a man a lot of work."

"I got an idea of how it functions. Would you be willing to share your plans or drawings?"

"Nope," Rudy seemingly objected. "I don't have any. Never did."

"Really? How about your torque conversions—do you have the calculations?"

"Nope. Never had any."

"Well, how did you know what to do?"

This was the sinker. We onlookers knew the answer, but it made us smile to hear it every time. "I just knew," said Rudy. He wasn't grandstanding, seeking praise, or being ornery. It was so innocently the truth that it invariably left the visitor momentarily dumbfounded.

"Would it be all right if we talk about what you did to build it?"

"Nope. What would you like to discuss?"

"I saw a power take-off connection.[5] How'd you reduce its speed and generate torque?"

"I just put a Model A transmission[6] in between the PTO and the drums. When I need to pull heavy and slow, I shift down. Once the haystack is halfway up the bed, I shift up. Loads faster that way."

"Makes sense... I guess. How did you know a Model A transmission would work?"

"Hmmm. Can't say. I just did."

---

[5]   A power takeoff (or PTO) is a device for taking power from a machine or engine. On a tractor, it is usually a drive shaft emerging from the rear-end that rotates when engaged and when the engine is running. It is typically connected to other implements with a splined drive shaft.

[6]   Model A is shortened reference to a Model A Ford. It was first produced and sold by the Ford Motor Company in 1927 and replaced the Model T.

The comment perplexed the visitor. It was clear that he lacked confidence in the answer—and in his own ability to connect everything just right. But he was into it now. "What about those drums that apparently turn to wrap the wire cable? You make them?"

"Sorta. They came off an old..."

So it went: the drums, the hydraulic lifts, the steel frame, the axle with dual wheels, all came from discarded equipment, some from machinery Rudy saw or used while in the Army.

"Well, thanks for letting me see your invention. You planning to patent it?"

"Nope."

"Mind if I try building one?"

"Go ahead. It's not hard. It'll save you a lot of work."

That's when Tommy and the hired man backed into my corner of the shop. They laughed quietly but heartily. "Not hard to make. Ha! Good luck, Buddy," they muttered. "We hope it works for you." At those times, Tommy rather appreciated Rudy's nonlogical, intuitive ways.

A few years later International Harvester came out with a fancy haystack hauler. We preferred Rudy's—a spectacle, I suppose, but it worked. Over the years, I saw many spectacles: two tractors joined together pulling five cultivators arranged side by side, three side-delivery rakes mounted in series on WD-6 International,[7] a granary[8] placed on top of

---

[7] A WD-6 International is a tractor. Rudy's was likely a McCormick Deering Farmall International Super WD-6. It was diesel powered and manufactured by International Harvester, McCormick Deering division, in the early 1950s.

[8] A granary is a building used for storing grain.

the milk house (why carry grain when you have gravity?), and more, always something.

Rudy was brilliant, but he didn't know it. Actually, he did not successfully complete the eighth grade, so he had no reason to claim superior intelligence. Rather, he humbly invented and rebuild things to make the farm work.

Following Rudy's direction, the hired man arrived at the milk house the next morning while it was still dark. He relieved Rudy who stopped by the shop and took me from my resting place. From a drawer, he took one long-rifle cartridge. He knew that he would only get off one shot, even if he missed, because the fox, if it showed up, would scamper into a grain field before he could reload. But then, as you know, Rudy was not planning on missing.

At the time, the Quonset (as Rudy called it) held hay bales, stacked to the height of its windows on the south end—about fifteen feet up. From the window, one had a clear view of the lane, but a wild animal would not instinctively be wary of the upper part of a structure unless something caught its attention. Rudy intended to be in place, resting on the hay well before daylight, with me, waiting for the fox.

He climbed the hay bales, not an easy task for a man sporting an artificial limb. At the top, he used his pliers and knife to remove a window. Then he inserted the long-rifle round into my chamber, snapped the bolt action in place, and pulled back the firing pin. Not activating the safety so as to be ready in an instant, he laid me on a bale of hay, well within reach. Then he watched as the sun came up.

He did not have long to wait. With the dawning of a new day, a bouncy, bushy-tailed red fox emerged from the oat field, looked up and down the lane, and then scurried into its center. There he paused again, but not out of concern, more to feel his liberty in the open space. He began trotting down the lane toward the farmstead. In about thirty yards the lane's fence would join that of the sheep pasture where he supposedly would squeeze through the woven wire and advance to the broiler house.

Rudy saw it all. He calculated that he had about twenty seconds before the fox exited the lane. I felt his grip. Deliberately, but slowly, very slowly, Rudy raised me to the window and to his shoulder and cheek to sight in the fox. Early in the morning, any wind for the day had not yet picked up. Nothing there for which to adjust. The distance was neither close nor far for my work. So with his aiming eye, Rudy adjusted my position such that the top of my front sight aligned with the bottom of the "V" in my rear sight...with the fox beyond. "One shot," Rudy reminded himself.

The fox proceeded down the lane, occasionally stopping and then advancing forward again. This approach seemed to Rudy to be more instinctual than wariness of anything the fox saw. Suspecting an opportunity of only another ten yards, Rudy held his breath and squeezed my trigger ever so smoothly. *Bam!*

A neutral person, or a lover of wild animals, is not going to like this next part. If it wasn't your chickens—your family's food—that was being stolen, you would probably vote for the fox. Of course. But this is an account of farm life, and the animals around the farm were not anthropomorphic Disney-like characters. Some were varmints, nuisances. While a farmer might admire their natural beauty, he also recognized that their freedom ended where his detriments began.

The fox simply dropped. It dropped right where it had been last totting, and there it lay—quiet, motionless, dead.

Rudy laid me back on the hay bale and reinserted the window, using his pliers to tap in the securing nails. Then he carefully climbed down. I was placed back in the shop on the counter.

Electing to head to town for an early breakfast, Rudy slid into the Shotgun and drove down the driveway to the main road.

I quite imagined that as he passed the farmhouse, he slyly glanced at the window of the bedroom where Tommy was still asleep. With the corners of his mouth easing upward, he softly chuckled.

Crazy, huh? Crazy...like a fox.

Oh, by the way, did you answer that question I posed at the outset?

I'll give you another one: What's the difference between slyness and intuition when you're a fox?

CHAPTER SEVEN

MASKED BANDIT

Down the lane, and east of where it opened to the pasture, was an old wooden granary.[1] It had faded over the years, but its original red color remained distinguishable. It stood alone just outside the pasture fence amidst a patch of grass that Rudy never cultivated. Against a rugged pasture on one side and a grain field on the other, it cast various impressions. When the sun rose or set behind it, it projected stories of foregoing settlers making the best they could of prairie life. As such, it suggested strength and endurance, mixed with hardship and eventual resignation. When lit by the moon, it cast enchanting shadows projecting mystery and bedevilment.

In a strange way, it was picturesque. Like a photograph of an old barn in a gallery, the image arrested one's

---

[1]   A granary is a building used for storing grain.

attention and made one wonder at the stories it could tell. In that way, the granary reminded me of myself.

Actually, the granary was intriguing for everyone on the farm, partly because Rudy referred to it as the Quamme Place, although he offered no explanation. Who was Quamme? Did he have a family? Was he a homesteader or the son of a homesteader? What was it like for him to farm the prairie? What led to his departure—disease (possibly), bankruptcy (common, unfortunately), loneliness (who knows?), or a profitable sale (not likely)? One question that was easily answered was, why was the granary still standing when all the other Quamme buildings were gone?

The granary earned its keep. You see, when the farm yielded bumper crops, Rudy needed it to store surplus grain. (Naturally, if Rudy had a bumper crop, so did other farmers. Therefore, supply was up and grain prices were down. The common strategy was to store the grain until acceptable prices returned.) The best facilities were used for wheat, the main money crop. The second best was for barley. If a building was marginal but could hold grain and keep it dry, it was used for oats.

Thus, Rudy kept the Quamme granary, even though it was removed from the farmstead and deteriorating. If the crop looked promising at the end of the summer, Rudy directed the hired man and Tommy to prepare the structure for oats. They swept it clean, boarded up holes, patched the roof, and "laid in" the tongue and grooved retaining boards[2] for the individual grain bins. The granary had four

---

[2] Tongue and grooved boards have a protruding ridge cut into one edge and a receiving groove cut into the other. The edges of two boards fit together snugly and provide support along their length.

bins, two on each side with an aisle of approximately eight feet wide running down the middle. The aisle, and thus the granary, was secured by a large sliding door attached to rollers that hung on steel rails. The door and the aisle were accessed when loading and unloading grain. You might be interested in how this worked.

Grain was funneled into each bin through an opening in the roof—four bins equal four openings. Each opening was covered and wired shut when not in use. To fill the bins, a truck dumped grain into a hopper from which the grain was transported to an opening by an auger—a long steel tube in which snuggly fitting, screw-shaped fins welded to a rotating shaft conveyed the grain farther along with each turn.

As grain poured into a granary, it formed a cone-shaped pile. To level out the grain, thereby filling it full to the top edges, Tommy or the hired man climbed ladder steps in the aisle, constructed on the side of each bin. You are imagining this activity well if you hear the sounds of the churning auger and see grain dust wafting out the granary door.

With the grain bins filled, the aisle door was pushed in place and steel stakes were hammered into the ground to clamp its bottom firmly against the footings.[3] At each vertical edge of the door, halfway up, clasps were used to hold the edges tight against the exterior walls.[4] Through the

---

[3]   Footings are essentially the concrete features forming a foundation upon which a building is set.

[4]   A clasp is a device that holds objects together. On the granary door, each clasp consisted of two parts: a semicircular ring attached to the wall and flat metal strap with a slot attached to the door and aligned with the ring. A clasp was completed when an object, such as a steel bolt, was placed through the ring after the strap was fitted over it.

ring of one clasp, a steel bolt was inserted. In the other, a padlock was used. The granary was thus secured from the elements (wind, rain, snow) as well as from casual intruders (varmints, vandals, thieves).

But, alas, the granary was indeed infiltrated...by a thief, and in response I was dispatched with great haste. It was one of the few times when I sensed wariness, insecurity, and, dare I say, fear by those who handled me.

Here's what happened.

The Quamme granary was usually the last structure from which Rudy took oats. In fact, if oats were not needed, it might not be tapped for another year or two. By the way, I say "needed" because oats were used on Rudy's farm to feed the animals. If the supply of oats exceeded consumption in a given year, it was not yet needed.

(Skip this explanation if you want, but I will enlighten you a smidgen about oats. They're high in protein; thus, they generate growth in animals and contribute to their production. In the case of dairy cows, production means milk—more milk. In the case of sheep, it means lambs—healthy lambs. For hogs or steers, it means "fattening"—meat-building weight gain. To make oats more easily digested, and therefore more efficient, they are typically ground. In other words, they are run through a grinder. The result is called ground feed, because it is commonly fed to livestock.)

Late one spring, or maybe it was early summer, Tommy and Lenn, the hired man at that time, were sent to the Quamme Place to get a load of oats to grind for the milk cows. They headed down the lane with Tommy driving a yellow Minneapolis-Moline[5] and pulling a grain auger. Lenn followed in the Chevy pickup outfitted with its grain box. (The tractor not only transported the grain auger, but once the unit was positioned it also turned the auger's shaft with its power takeoff. The pickup hauled the grain to the elevator[6] in town where the oats were ground and reloaded into its box.)

Nothing looked amiss when Tommy and Lenn reached the granary. The roof openings were covered, the stakes were secure, and the clasps were fastened. Yet, upon pushing the door open, Tommy and Lenn sensed something ominous. Tommy expressed concern. "Something seems wrong. You feeling this, too?"

"I am," said Lenn. "Let's look around."

He climbed the wall and looked over the grain. "An animal's been in here. It's ruining the grain. There's scat all over."

"Really?" questioned Tommy. "Let me look." He climbed up also. "Whew! A fairly big animal. And some of its droppings are fresh."

---

[5] The Minneapolis-Moline was a tractor produced by a company of the same name—the result of an early-century merger of Minneapolis Steel and Machinery, Minneapolis Threshing Machine, and Moline Plow. Yellow was its distinctive color. Rudy's tractor had two narrowly spaced, tricycle wheels and a hand clutch.

[6] An elevator is complex for managing grain. It can be used to weigh, purchase, clean, store, grind, and transport grain. Typically, this complex has a tower containing a bucket elevator that moves grain from lower to higher levels. From the higher levels, shoots may send grain to connected storage units.

"Get back!" yelled Lenn. "There's something in here. Way back in the corner."

"What is it?"

"Don't know. Open the door all the way for more light."

Tommy jumped down, pushed the door fully open, and climbed back up. Both peered at a shadow in the back corner. It moved!

Good grief! What if it's a badger? thought Tommy. *It could attack and tear a person, or parts of a person, to shreds.*

Lenn was having similar thoughts. The shadow spun and stared straight at them. The animal was a...thief! Well, it was wearing a black mask, or so it appeared. A raccoon.[7]

"It's a coon," pronounced Lenn, jumping down, followed by Tommy.

"So, what shall we do?"

"I'm not sure."

"Maybe we could bang on the granary walls and scare it out."

"Then it'll be back another time and create more problems."

"Yeah, we better shoot it."

"Okay," said Lenn. "Let's seal up this place and get the .22."

Hurriedly they secured the granary, hopped in the pickup, and drove back up the lane to the shop. On the way, Tommy asked the question each had been considering. "How did the raccoon get in there?"

---

[7] Raccoons typically have black fur around their eyes, contrasting with the rest of the face. The result looks like a mask.

"Beats me. The door was tight when we arrived," replied Lenn.

"That's the way I saw it, too. Mice could get in or perhaps a weasel, but nothing as big as a raccoon."

"Yeah," Lenn agreed. "The roof covers were in place, too."

"Very perplexing," said Tommy.

Lenn changed their focus. "When we get back there, I don't figure that coon's going to be as still as she was. She knows we spotted her, so I doubt she'll continue hiding."

"You're probably right. What are we going to do? I don't want to be in that granary with a raccoon tearing around in a wild frenzy. Maybe I should just pound on the walls to scare it out, and when it flees, you can shoot it."

"I don't think that'll work. That critter is going to be flying when it decides to run. With a single shot, I don't have much of a chance. And besides, the tall grass around the granary will make a clear shot difficult."

"Should we get Dad to help?"

"No. This is our job. He sent us for the oats."

"Okay. What are we going to do? I'm not facing a terrified raccoon at close range."

They were at the shop and yet without a plan. They only knew they were going to put me to work. Lenn pulled me from the counter. Tommy rummaged through drawers to find a flashlight and a few .22 "shorts"[8]—plenty of firepower for close range. Why a few? I don't know, because as

---

[8] "Short" .22 cartridges are the smallest of .22 ammunition rounds. It was generally regarded that shorts, when shot level to the ground, would travel one-half mile.

Lenn said after I shot once the raccoon would be free if it was a miss. Well, I suppose they could wound it, and then I would have to shoot again.

Driving back down the lane, Lenn articulated what he thought was the best approach. He would stand ready while Tommy cracked open the door. If the coon stayed inside, he'd look in to determine where it was holed up and its disposition. Hopefully, it would still be hunkered shyly in a corner. If the coon was "on the move," they would block the door and wait for it to settle down. Then Tommy was to shine a light on the animal. If it didn't bolt, Lenn would shoot it.

The way I pictured it, the coon, as Lenn called it, would look into the light, from behind its mask. With its eyes shining, Lenn would have a clear target. Tommy simply had to hold the light steady.

Steady? He wasn't feeling steady. To the contrary. He had dealt with domestic animals gone wild—hogs and a bull, for sure. That was unpleasant, to put it mildly. Picturing a wild animal gone wild, frankly, was beyond his imagination. Thus, he was, shall I say, unsettled.

They parked the pickup. Lenn popped in a cartridge, grabbed my bolt, and leveraged the firing assembly in place. Pulling back the firing pin, he said, "Okay, open the door. Just a little. And keep that coon in there. Be ready to close it again."

Tommy did as commanded, keeping one eye on the opening and one eye on Lenn. He wished Lenn had set the safety because if he was equally nervous this showdown could get extra messy—a wayward shot could hit anything or anybody. But Tommy realized that there wouldn't be time to flip the safety lever if the coon burst through the door.

The raccoon did not bolt.

Tommy held the flashlight in the door and followed its light, looking around. No raccoon, but then it was likely high on top of the grain and likely in a corner. Lenn squeezed through the door's opening, holding me tightly though nervously. Then Tommy squeezed in. They climbed a bin wall, and Tommy held the flashlight over Lenn's shoulder. He flashed it from corner to corner. Lenn tried pointing me to keep up with the light, but it moved too quickly. "Don't flash the light so fast! You'll scare her," he barked abruptly, displaying his own trepidation.

"Sorry." With that Tommy shined the light slowly along one wall, then another, then along the back wall. Nothing.

"Aim the light in the corners. Start on the left," Lenn harshly commanded, his anxiety peaking.

Tommy took no offense. Being tense was to be expected. He did as directed. Nothing. "Maybe she burrowed into the grain."

No such sign.

They began to relax. Tommy opened the door to max-imize daylight in the granary. Ready to shoot, Lenn again inspected along the walls, in the corners, and within the grain itself. The masked bandit was gone! Gone. It had vanished.

How? How did it get out?

But then, how? How did it get in?

No one—not Tommy, the hired man, Rudy, or the Little Brothers—could come up with a plausible theory.

———————————

The Quamme granary continued to weather the years. And on it, the sun's shadows continued to speak stories; the moon's, mystery.

CHAPTER EIGHT

REARMED

You cannot appreciate North Dakota farm life without comprehending winter on the northern plains.[1] It truly takes a toll on life and limb. Limb? you ask warily. Yes, but not another of Rudy's. Tommy's—his arm, his preferred right hand. I was held in his left, seconds before he was shot.

Let me be clear: I did not shoot him. When the scene calmed, I was found on the shop floor with my wing safety secure, restraining my firing pin. So, I am not at fault. Tommy agrees. He blamed winter and still does.

Winters in North Dakota are cold. Oh, they can have warm days and may include a January thaw. For sure, if that comes, don't count on it to last long. Standard winters see temperatures frequently below zero, way below. Rudy

---

[1] The northern plains are the flatlands of the Northern United States. They are part of the interior plains but not necessarily part of the Great Plains. Prairies are grassy ecoregions on the plains.

checked his thermometer every morning when he rose before 5:00. He once reported that he had not seen the mercury[2] for three straight weeks. Shutter with me when I tell you that the mercury in his thermometer shrunk below its plastic molding and out of sight at −25°F. Others whose thermometers were readable at extreme temperatures reported mornings below −30°F. For anyone, these fiercely frigid days were troublesome; for those tending livestock they were dreadful; for Rudy who had a dairy, they were destructive, and at times deadly.

First, destructive: when Rudy rose in the dark, motionless mornings, he might find frozen water fountains, although they were ostensibly warmed by heating elements and electric tape. All livestock need water, and dairy cows require large amounts to produce milk. Thus, making the fountains operable was a top priority. In the intense cold, the job was miserable and could occupy hours for Rudy and the hired man.

As you can imagine the subzero temperatures affected everything mechanical. Anything made of cast iron was extremely brittle. Tommy learned this the hard way when he pounded on a cast water handle at the well to force it open. It shattered. More problems, then. To get vehicles and motorized equipment started, such as tractors, Rudy "plugged them in" hours before planning to use them. "Plugging in" involves running electricity via an extension

---

[2] Mercury was commonly used in mercury-in-glass thermometers during the 1950s. Due to its high toxicity, other chemicals have typically replaced mercury in modern thermometers.

cord to the vehicle and its head bolt or tank heater.[3] Either mechanism warms an engine by heating its coolant. (Antifreeze, it's often called, with good reason.)

In the extreme cold, the teats[4] of some of the cows were injured—frostbit or fully frozen. Rudy thawed them carefully and applied healing salve. Infection, nonetheless, often developed, requiring him to inject antibiotics into just the udder or into the flank or rump of the cow.

As to deadly, the cold created distress for calves. If a mother cow appeared ready to freshen[5] during a spell of low temperatures, Rudy moved her to a separate section of a barn. There she had a clean, obstacle-free environment for calving, but she lacked the warmth generated by other animals. The newborn calf truly entered a cold world. But it was not cruel. In addition to the care the mother provided, Rudy, the hired man, Tommy, or the Little Brothers intervened to seal the barn from the outdoors, scatter clean straw for bedding, and assist the calf in sucking its mother's milk.

Still, the arctic air attacked and sometimes conquered the little ones. In other words, not all survived. Some succumbed in their first days; others later, when separated from their mothers.

After a calf's first week, Rudy moved it to the calf barn.

---

[3] A head bolt heater is an engine block heater. A heating element is typically installed to replace one of the plugs in the engine's core. There the coolant is warmed. Tank heaters perform similarly, although they are installed in cooling system hoses.

[4] A cow's teats are the projections from her udders or mammary glands. From teats, milk is ejected.

[5] Freshen means to become fresh. Cows are said to freshen when they have a calf and then begin to produce milk.

There the cold also wreaked havoc, both directly and indirectly. Hyperthermia directly dealt its blows during bitter nights. Because the cold forced Rudy to congregate the calves in a barn, they, unfortunately, transmitted to one another viral diseases and bacterial infections. Sadly, pneumonia required Rudy's vigilance. When its symptoms were evident, he directed the hired man or others to administer penicillin. Sometimes it was effective, and the calf later enjoyed the freshness of spring.

As merciless as the cold was, its description fails to convey the full story of winter, at least on the North Dakota prairie where the wind is a major concern. It penetrates otherwise protective buildings and clothing to amplify the cold. Wind chill[6] temperatures of −50°F are common. Minus 70°F and minus 90°F were reported at times. On occasion, the radio reported on travelers who were stranded when their vehicles malfunctioned during windy winter nights. Of course, if it's radio news, you can expect a fateful outcome: overexposure was the usual pronouncement.

Worse was the combination of wind and snow. On the prairie, after it snows once, the snow can blow for weeks with the changing wind. One day it blows the snow east, the next south. Rare, but possible, is snow blowing westerly from an eastern wind. With blowing snow came snow drifts that formed in untoward locations, such as over roadways or along feed bunks for the livestock. They can be deep,

---

[6] Wind chill or wind chill factor measures the extent that wind lowers body temperature. With wind, especially moist wind, the temperature feels colder than it actually is. Wind chill increases the rate of heat loss. Formulas to calculate wind chill vary.

and hard—in other words, dangerous. When necessary, Rudy, or the hired man, busted them apart with a tractor equipped with a front-end loader.

On the plains, wind is more feared when accompanied by falling snow. Visibility can be obliterated. Tales were told of hapless souls losing their bearings going from their barn to the farmhouse during a whiteout.[7] After the storm passed, the doomed farmer, or his assisting son or daughter, was discovered, sometimes a half mile away—"overexposure" is again a fitting euphemism. So it was that people of the prairie imagined the terror of becoming disoriented and then not stumbling into the house or barn, but instead just stumbling.

As a precaution, some farmers of old strung a wire between buildings to guide passage. Rudy did not. But he had stern guidance. "Listen, Sons," he said with an expression and tone that commanded attention. "If it's storming and you're heading out to help, you watch behind you. If the house is getting faint before you see the shop, turn back and wait for the wind to die down. Same, from the shop to the barn." He did not elaborate. He didn't need to. The boys had heard the stories of others' missteps; thus, instructions for preserving their lives required no repetition.

If you're bored by these accounts of winter, skip ahead, but out of respect for Tommy and the tragedy he blamed on the heartless season, I have a few more things to say.

Wind and snow mixed are ruthless—deathly ruthless,

---

[7]   A whiteout from snowfall or blowing snow occurs when visibility is reduced to practically zero. In a complete whiteout, one cannot see objects several feet away.

at times—and their effect is exacerbated when they arise unexpectedly, as when some storm surprises farmers in the fall, theoretically, before winter arrives—or in the spring, theoretically, after winter passes. Unprotected livestock suffers horribly. Herds of cattle will walk with the wind until they reach a fence where they are stopped.[8] There the wet snow of a fall or spring surprise drenches them, the wind pierces hair and hide, and the falling temperatures finish them off. Hundreds, even thousands, of cattle die from these untimely winter events.

More than once, Tommy hastened in a pickup to the east pasture to round up the cattle and "push" them into the west wind. They balked because the wind assailed their bodies and the blowing snow slashed their eyes. Yet, Tommy forced their advance until they reached the shelter of the farmstead where they were spared.

So it is that winter is much more than one of four seasons. It is the season to which all others submit. The spring with all its welcoming would hardly appeal if it were not for the escape of winter's grasp. It evidences the aftermath of winter and then spawns new plant life, much of which is later harvested to get through the next winter. In the summer farmers like Rudy prepare hay to nourish livestock during the long, cold, and dark months. In the fall, grain is thrashed, corn is cut for silage,[9] and both are hauled to

---

[8] In a storm, cattle tend to walk in the direction of the wind.

[9] Rudy's silage was comprised of chopped corn leaves, stalks, and ears and was compacted and stored in a pit without being dried. A layer of hay or straw bales was stacked on the silage to help preserve the top several inches.

the farmstead because everyone knows it's coming. Yes "it." Winter is so respected that folks don't have to name it to discuss it. Instead, you hear things like: "It was a tough one." "I haven't seen many pheasants this summer, it probably got them." "It will be here soon."

"It" requires diversion. Tommy primarily focused on basketball. After all, it's an indoor sport. But he also tried to accept winter and outdoor recreation. When he was thirteen years old and in the eighth grade, Tommy, along with his friend Johnny, took up hunting on warmer days—in other words, less cold ones.

Johnny had a .410 pump-style shotgun[10]and Tommy had me. Rudy cautioned them about inherent dangers of firearms and showed them standard handling procedures. He elaborated on using safety mechanisms until taking aim. "Had better be safe even if the game gets away," he cautioned. The boys acknowledged and dutifully followed his advice.

To reach the tree rows where they would hunt for rabbits, Tommy and Johnny fashioned a sleigh from an overturned 1953 Packard hood with its ornament removed.[11] It was drawn over the snow by Johnny's three-year-old mare, named Star. (What else would you name a horse that was completely black except for a white spot on its forehead?) She was quite gentle for her age and "took" to the harness

---

[10] A .410 shotgun is a smaller shotgun. Its bore, or gauge, accommodates a bullet (slug) of .410 inches in diameter. It is referred to as a "four-ten."

[11] Packard cars were manufactured in the 1950s by the Packard Motor Car Company of Detroit, Michigan.

splendidly. With some training she soon learned to trot through the snow, pulling the boys along. She was a keeper, and with Rudy's permission, they arranged to board her on the farm. (Horses were no longer used for farming, but Rudy's barn was erected in a previous era and had stalls complete with feed mangers.)

One afternoon in late February, the temperature was unusually mild—in the lower 30s—and Johnny, driven to the farm by his father, asked Tommy if he'd be interested in hunting rabbits until dusk. Tommy agreed.[12] They harnessed Star, hitched up the hood, and climbed aboard with their guns and ammunition. Across the road they went and over several snow drifts until they reached a row of trees. There they tethered the mare and set out on foot with their firearms. After walking for a half mile and not seeing any game, they reversed direction and hiked back.

Because the tree row had already been explored, the chance of scaring up a rabbit was practically nil. Tommy and Johnny checked us firearms to make sure our safeties were on. Then they relaxed and commenced a youthful conversation. For some foreshadowing reason, they talked about hunting accidents.

---

[12] Tommy was actually stranded at home, missing a high school basketball game, the first in which he was invited to participate although he was only in the eighth grade. He was unaware the opponent was a Canadian team, requiring the game to be played in the late afternoon, so the visitors could return before the border closed. Consequently, he did not bring his gear to school. Upon arriving home on the bus, no one was available to take him back to town for the game.

Tommy asked, "Have you ever thought about what it would feel like to be shot?"

"Quite a bit, I'd have to say," replied Johnny. "After seeing two others get shot this fall, it's been on my mind." (Johnny didn't actually "see" the shootings, and Tommy knew what he meant.)

"Yeah, same here. Everyone says the river kid was trying to kill a varmint when he had his accident. Is that what you heard?"

"Sorta. Somebody said he was after a cougar. That would get a person pretty nervous."

"It would have me shaking in my boots, that's for sure. But I'm guessing that's just people talking. Who knows how he got killed?" The question was only rhetorical. You see the river kid had been new to the school, joining in the fall for a high school education. The boys knew only what was relayed by the school authorities and that the young man was never seen again. Sad.

Moving on, Johnny stated, "My friend's brother was just shot through the hand. Everything healed quickly."

"So, what happened?" asked Tommy.

"He says he was carrying a .22, and it went off."

"How did it hit his hand? What side did it go through?"

"It went through his palm and out the back. He says that he was just carrying it and it went off."

"Was he carrying it with his hand over the end of the barrel?"

"Maybe."

"Pretty dumb, if that's the case," declared Tommy.

Johnny simply replied, "It was an accident," as if to say, things happen that aren't anticipated and can't be explained.

By the time they reached Star, Tommy's hands had grown stiff from the cold. Because it was a relatively warm afternoon when they started out, he had elected to wear gloves. Though insulated, they were not as warm as mittens, but they were more functional when handling me. Wearing gloves, Tommy could easily insert rounds of ammunition, lever my bolt in place, ready the firing pin, and activate the safety. When the temperature dropped with the setting sun, his fingers suffered. For a while, they stung, and then they went numb. So it was that Johnny drove[13] Star back over the snowdrifts and back into the farmyard while Tommy held us firearms on his lap.

At the shop, Johnny stopped the mare with a "Whoa" and a gentle pull on the reins. "How about you put the guns away, and I'll take care of the horse? I'll meet you in the house."

"Okay," agreed Tommy. "Help me get one over each shoulder."

"Sure. Can you put them on the counter by yourself?"

"Oh, yeah. I can still grip with my left hand."

Johnny propped me upright, against Tommy's parka with my barrel over his shoulder and the butt of my stock in his left hand. Johnny similarly placed the shotgun on Tommy's right.

"You sure they are on safety?" Tommy asked, even

---

[13] To drive a horse is to guide and control it with long reins while it is hitched by a harness to a wagon, sleigh, plow, etc.

though he could see that they were. Johnny checked and Tommy started walking to the shop, carrying the firearms, soldier style. With a "Giddy-up" Johnny headed for the barn.

It was only about twelve steps to the shop, but they were over ice and hardpack snow. Tommy proceeded carefully. He pushed the side door of the shop open with a foot. Then he stepped up to cross the threshold.

His movements caused us firearms to slightly shuffle. In his left hand he felt me slipping. He adjusted his position to steady me against his coat. In this he was successful, but his attention was diverted from his very cold, non-feeling right hand. The .410 slid out.

When the shotgun's butt hit the concrete floor, it went off. Birdshot fired upward, grazing Tommy's right cheek and plastering the top of the door frame.[14] I fell to the floor in a clatter. With his ears ringing from the blast, Tommy, feeling the scratches on his face, rubbed it with the back of his gloved left hand, the one less affected by the cold. No blood. He breathed to himself, "I was lucky."

He stooped to pick me up, and then he saw it. The end of his right forearm was hanging perpendicular to the remainder. Flesh and blood were mixed with shredded cloth. In a panic, he yelled, "I got hit! I got hit!" (Later Johnny reported hearing Tommy cry out, "I got it! I got it!" He assumed Tommy wasn't that cold after all and had taken an opportunity to shoot a sparrow.)

Gripped by shock, Tommy grabbed his dangling arm

---

[14] Shotgun .410 gauge shells are usually loaded with birdshot pellets, which are smaller than buckshot pellets. Pellets, also called shot, are spherical and made of metal.

and began running to the house. As he rounded the shop's corner, he saw Mother drive up with an elderly couple in her car. Seeing them, he somehow derived that his mangled arm might frighten the couple, so he turned his back to shield it from their view. Mother, however, saw Tommy' anguish, jumped from the car, and rushed him into the house.

Rudy had come home earlier and was already in the house along with Sister and the Little Brothers. To them, Mother screamed for help. Rudy called a doctor. Mother pulled dish towels from a drawer and with them wrapped Tommy's arm along with the sleeve of his parka. Sister and the Little Brothers could only look on in sympathy—well, perhaps it was empathy, because their countenances, like Tommy's, displayed horrid distress. Everyone prayed.

(The arm, although shot just behind the wrist, did not bleed profusely, and Tommy only had minor pain. Not what you'd expect. Later a doctor theorized that because Tommy's arm was close to the fired gun barrel, its flame cauterized the wound. As to limited pain, he had a convincing explanation: the nerves were severed.)

Rudy rushed out to fuel up the car, and then he, with Mother and Tommy, raced to the hospital—forty miles away. I was not surprised to find out that Rudy drove over the speed limit. Mother asked him to slow down because they might get arrested. Interestingly, that is what Rudy hoped for. At the time, the family car was faithful but old, and it lacked integrity required for a sustained high speed. It began to overheat, and Rudy saw the temperature needle move into the red. He blurted, "Right now, I want a patrolman. This kid needs to get to a doctor." None appeared.

Mother decided to leave the driving to Rudy. She turned to Tommy. "We have always trusted God to take care of us. He will now, too. Your arm looks bad, but God can heal it. Do you think he can?"

Tommy had no doubts. "Yes," he replied, looking into Mother's eyes.

They prayed that Tommy's arm would one day be restored. Of course, that prayer gives God a lot of "room," because, in the end, He could restore the arm in heaven. But their faith was not for a time later in eternity. It was for a life on Earth.

The doctor at the hospital knew Rudy and that he had learned to live with an artificial limb. Thus, after visually examining the arm, he took Rudy aside to confidentially share his grim assessment. "Rudy, it's a mess; the only thing I can do is amputate."

"Doc, that's not an option. Tommy's going to have both his arms."

"I'm sorry, Rudy. I can't do anything else."

"Who can?"

"Maybe another physician, a specialist. I can phone ahead. It's another fifty miles."

"You call. I'll get Tommy and the wife."

Actually, Rudy also made a quick call. He rang up a nearby relative and asked to borrow his car. With it, they drove on to the big city. There an orthopedic specialist was waiting. Although alarmed by the severity of the injury, he rendered care confident that he could save the arm. In a couple of hours, he cut off the parka, cleaned the wound, and arranged for surgery. It would be the first of five.

During the second checkup after the first surgery, the orthopedist performed a routine examination. "Try wiggling your fingers."

Tommy obliged.

"You have a little movement. Good." The doc went on, "With therapy, it will improve."

It was not much upon which to base hope, but Tommy did.

"Try your thumb. Press it against my hand."

Tommy tried.

"Well, Son, it's probably not significant to you, but I am encouraged. It will get better also." With that, he took a safety pin from his drawer and poked the top of Tommy's wrist. "I need to do this for a complete examination, but I know you can't feel it." He reached for his ink pen to write a note in his record book.

"Doc," squeaked Tommy. "I felt that."

"Couldn't have. I never worked on the nerve fibers. In several years they should grow back."

"I felt it! I felt the pin on the back of my hand."

"No. Let's do it again. Close your eyes and tell me when and where I poke."

The physician was astounded! He ran to find his associate to show him the remarkable recovery.

Tommy knew that if God had done the harder thing, He would heal the bones and flesh, as well. But that did not come without trials. As I mentioned, four additional surgeries were necessary. When Tommy finally had use of his arm, two more winters had passed.

Compared to Tommy's left, his new arm was not attractive, nor strong, nor dexterous, but it testified to what a good doctor and a gracious God can do.

During the healing years, Johnny acquired other friends and interests that did not include horses. Except for shooting gophers, Tommy seldom hunted again.

Things changed for me, as well: I was moved to the milk house where Rudy thought I would be more accessible. Because he regarded me as merely a tool, it never occurred to him to fault me—or anyone else, for that matter—for Tommy's accident. I wish it hadn't happened, and I, too, know I was not to blame.

CHAPTER NINE

MARAUDERS

One of my jobs was to protect the sheep. Early one morning I was summoned to do this in a dramatic and deadly fashion. With Rudy's steady aim, I saved hundreds of sheep. But then, too, I created several enemies for Rudy—folks who, until then, were his closest friends.

———————

I confess: regarding sheep, I have mixed sentiments. I suppose I have been influenced by Tommy's opinion. He disliked sheep most of the time and claimed to find them flatly contemptible. Yet he, too, would admit to occasionally having positive emotions for them, especially when they were mistreated.

Sheep are dumb. I don't mean they can't hear, although they might as well not, considering how they ignore yelling, horns, and whistles. I mean they are stupid. Well, they come off as stupid, because they act self-sufficient when in reality they can do very little for themselves. Without the animal husbandry[1] provided by humans, they could not survive.

Consider a few points. One, they eat grass—the grass they prefer, that is—down to the nub. Other perfectly nutritious grass goes untouched. With hot or dry days—or worse, the combination of hot and dry—the grass dies. Then what do the dumb sheep have to eat?

Two, they grow wool. Impressive, yes, but they can't shed it, so with hot weather they would suffer severely. Only with humans, intervening to shear off the wool, are they viable.

One more: they follow each other blindly. (And interestingly, with a little training, they will even follow a person, which Tommy can attest to, as you will see.) This "blind" patterning is humorous at times. For example, when sheep have become accustomed to a fully enclosed fence, they require patient persuasion to get them through a gate that has been opened. You can herd them next to the gate where they'll stand bleating away, as though in a death trap. Eventually, one processes the reality that the gate is open, and, fancy that, an alternative exists. Does the sheep then run through? No! It cautiously eyes the line where the gate once was. Then it jumps over the line to freedom, acting victorious. Voila, you dumb sheep. You never leaped over anything! Blindly following, the remaining sheep—Rudy had about 500 head—all jump or hop over "the line," just like the ones before them. The only exception is sheep

---

[1]   Animal husbandry is the aspect of agriculture involving the production and care of domesticated animals.

too old to jump. Believe me, watching them try is painfully exasperating.

On the other hand, the innocence of sheep makes them endearing. You sort of, dare I say, love them. The Bible compares people to sheep. Maybe we humans, in God's eyes, are dumb, falsely self-sufficient, and given to destroying the environment that sustains us. And maybe we, like sheep, are hopeless without a good shepherd.[2]

Rudy was the sheep's shepherd.[3] As mentioned before, he counted them coming through the lane to ensure all were home safely after a day of open grazing. He provided shelter and feed throughout the winter. Without these, the sheep would never have negotiated the deep snow that often covered the prairie. He also aided their lambing,[4] sheared their wool, and counteracted deadly disease. These intercessions warrant elaboration—before I describe for you the marauders and their merciless attack.

Rudy introduced rams—he called them bucks[5]—to the sheep band[6] each September, to time the lambing process for the late winter.[7] With this programming, he could fully focus on the sheep before spring work, when he was busy preparing the fields for sowing.[8] Moreover, the February–

---

[2] See for example Psalm 23 and Isaiah 53.

[3] A shepherd is a person who takes care of sheep.

[4] Lambing is the time or process of sheep birthing lambs.

[5] Rams are male sheep. They are also called bucks, a slang term.

[6] A band is a large group of sheep. Smaller groups are called flocks.

[7] The gestation period for sheep is usually a little less than five months, although the actual average varies a few days by sheep breed.

[8] Sowing is the act of disseminating seeds in the earth. It is a form of planting.

March schedule gave the lambs two additional months of growth before being sold in the fall. (The ram lambs—wethers by then[9]—were always sold; ewe lambs might be marketed, but many were retained to restock the herd.)

Lambing indeed summoned Rudy's attention. In preparation, he built pens along the insides of the Quonset. Each pen was large enough to hold a ewe and her young—twins were common and triplets were not rare. Above the enclosure, Rudy hung a heat lamp and plugged it in when the pen was in use. At the end of the Quonset that had large doors, Rudy stacked bales,[10] negating the use of the doors but maximizing space. Hay bales were for feeding and straw for bedding.[11] To bed down the sheep Rudy cut open the bales of straw and spread it for the animals to lie upon. Interestingly, the straw bales also comprised Rudy's bed during the heart of lambing.

He slept in the Quonset, warmed by heat lamps. Every hour or so, he would rise to walk among the sheep, looking for ewes going into labor. Finding one, he would move her into a pen. Occasionally, a ewe experienced trouble birthing. Then Rudy played the role of a midwife—to use a human term—assisting in delivery. It was exhausting work from which he occasionally needed a break.

One Thursday evening during the latter days of lambing, Mother asked Rudy to accompany her to a prayer meeting. Rudy obliged, putting Tommy in charge of the sheep. Given

---

[9]   Wethers are castrated male sheep.

[10] Bales are compressed material secured by wires, bands, string, or cords.

[11] Straw is the dry stalks of grain after it has been thrashed.

what occurred later, you will probably conclude that it was good that Rudy and Mother were praying.

It was well after dark when they returned. Driving down the road they spotted a yellow-orange glow in the vicinity of the Quonset. Closer, they realized the glow was from a fire. One side of the Quonset was in flames. A heat lamp apparently malfunctioned. Rushing into the house, Mother screamed, "Tommy, go help Dad. The sheep barn is on fire."

Then she grabbed the telephone to call for assistance, hoping volunteer firefighters could be assembled in time to save the sheep. But such hope was not realistic. The family was likely on its own.

Tommy grabbed his coat, sprinted to the Quonset, and dashed through its side door. Rudy had opened it and was frantically chasing the sheep, struggling to get them to exit. Still in his "church" clothes, of course, Rudy yelled for help, which he clearly needed. Tommy, however, doubted his assistance would be sufficient.

The sheep, acting normal—dumb, that is—would not recognize or accept the fact that the door was open. The fire was spreading. Its smoke was stifling, and before long, it would be suffocating. Could just one sheep recognize that the door was open and that egress meant safety? Finally, a brave soul ventured a jump into the night. Then another, and another.

Now eager to get out, the sheep bunched at the door. But it takes 500 sheep a long time to press through a side door made originally for only human passage. And long is longer when inside a building that is on fire!

Down to about 100 head yet to escape, Rudy yelled to Tommy, "That's it. We have to get out!" Smoke had increased in quantity and was threateningly black. Now intent on preserving their own lives, they climbed through and over the remaining sheep to reach the door. As they emerged, they heard the siren of a fire engine. Thank you, God!

Rudy and the hired man patched up the Quonset. In a couple of months, it was used for shearing just as it had in the years before the fire. Sheep shearing was a complex operation, involving persons to herd and catch sheep, to shear, to gather wool, to pack wool, and to supply a lunch in the morning, dinner at noon, and another lunch in the afternoon. Of course, such complexity required supervising and occasional expediting. That's where Rudy came in. With the size of his band, the whole operation took two to four days, depending on the number of shearers who were hired.

A small corral was constructed. In it, a flock of fifteen to twenty sheep from the larger band were enclosed. Because the pen was small, a person could corner a sheep, and then grab it by its wool, flip it onto its haunches, and drag it to a shearer. This was Tommy's favorite job—probably because he could "legally" "be rough" on his four-legged "friends." Unfortunately for him, however, he was usually assigned to packing wool.

After each sheep was sheared, its wool was gathered into a bundle and tied with twine.[12] The bundle was then tossed into a huge gunnysack, about two and one half feet in diameter and nine feet long. The sack was hung from

---

[12] Twine is a light string made of twisted fiber strands.

an elevated front-end loader. After several bundles were thrown into the sack, Tommy climbed the loader, slid along its arms, and jumped in. There he stomped down the wool to compress it and tightly fill the sack. As bundles were added, the bottom rose until Tommy was near the top. When full, the sack was sewn shut and stacked on a truck along with others. In time they were transported to the market.

Compressing the wool was not a pleasant task. The wool was often oily, especially that from near a sheep's skin. Worse, the wool might have crawling ticks, parasites looking for a new host. Oh, well. At least Tommy was part of the operation, and it felt good to be included, even though most of the day could be spent down in a sack. To alleviate the isolation, he would enlist the assistance of one of the Little Brothers. Together they packed the wool, and while waiting for another bundle to arrive they tussled, told jokes, and otherwise acted silly. There always seemed to be a way to make work fun.

To prevent disease, the sheep also required the husbandry of a shepherd.

Thus, Rudy had standard operating procedures for the lambs soon after they were born. All lambs were docked; the males were also castrated. Docking was important because it headed off disease—well, infection.

Hang with me. You're about to get some frank farmer talk, although I'll try to keep it tame. With docking, I'm referring to the practice of shortening lambs' tails. This is mostly done to reduce the chance of feces accumulating on the hindquarters and thereby reduce the chance of fly-strike. I'll explain. Parasitic flies are inclined to lay eggs in residual excrement on sheep. When they hatch, maggots grow and bury themselves in the wool. They may infest the skin and feed off the sheep's flesh. Infection likely sets in.

Disgusting, yes, and deadly. So a shepherd takes the precautionary procedure of docking lambs' tails. In Rudy's case, he banded each lamb's tail two to three days after birth, right before he turned the ewe and its offspring out of a birthing pen. He used a tool called an elastrator to stretch open a rubber band, slide it over the tail's end and upward to leave only a few inches, and then release the band. This method (compared to others) was relatively painless, and within ten days the tail fell off. (Male lambs were castrated at the same time and with the same method.)

Shearing, which I have already described, also helps prevent fly-strike. So does dipping. To protect sheep from mites, ticks, and lice, they are dipped into (or sprayed with) a liquid containing insecticide and fungicide. Rudy simply filled a large galvanized tank with the solution. The sheep were corralled and then one at a time caught and dipped. It was manual labor, but for Tommy, it was enjoyable, probably because it afforded him another excuse to manhandle the "dumb critters," as he put it.

In truth Tommy, too, had duplicitous feelings concerning the sheep. When he heard of how they had been savaged the morning of the attack, he was distraught—incensed with the assailants and downhearted when considering the brutality the sheep suffered. You see, he once had a pet lamb, and memory of its loyalty prompted genuine sympathy.

Yes, a pet lamb. During lambing one winter when Tommy was quite young—probably age five or six—a mother ewe regrettably died while birthing her baby. Rudy tried to get another ewe to "adopt" the orphan, but none would, although Rudy had been successful in this endeavor at other times. He brought the "bum" lamb to the farmhouse and asked Mother if she and Tommy would rescue it. They agreed, and the lamb was taken to the basement where they fed it with a bottle. Having the newborn sucking life from the bottle he was holding made Tommy feel valued. Perhaps he and the bum bonded.

After a couple of weeks, the lamb was moved to a barn where Tommy continued to provide care. It had a black face—Rudy had several sheep with that marking—and Tommy called it Blackie. He had a pet. In the spring it began following him wherever he went on the farmstead. This practice extended into the summer, with the lamb continuing to grow. Visitors would chuckle at the large lamb tagging little Tommy as he played on the lawn, pulled his wagon down the driveway, or wandered by the shop to see what the men were up to. At some point, it was introduced to the sheep band where it fit in quite naturally.

(In passing I might mention that this lamb was taken to market along with others in the fall. They were loaded unto train cars and transported to the big city. Rudy rode along to ensure none suffocated in route. When sold, Blackie brought $12, a smart sum in the mid-50's. Mother suggested saving that money for college. They stored it in a sugar jar for a couple of years before depositing it in a bank. About thirteen years later, when Tommy boarded an airplane for college, his family—Rudy, Mother, Sister, and the Little Brothers—stood on the tarmac and hugged Tommy goodbye. In his hands was the receipt for the plane ticket... paid for by Blackie.)

The morning of the marauders started like any typical summer day. Rudy rose early (about 4:45), rounded up the cows, and began milking. About 6:30 he was interrupted by a neighboring farmer who rushed into the milking parlor exceedingly alarmed. He blurted out that while driving past Rudy's far pasture he witnessed a pack of dogs attacking the sheep. Something needed to be done! Rudy was "on it."

Moving quickly as he could, he released the cows being milked and pulled me down from the nails upon which I rested above a window. (After Tommy's winter accident, I was moved to the milk house to be more accessible—a good thing.)

From a shelf, Rudy also pulled a box of ammunition—long rifle, hollow points.[13] I was being called upon to kill with certainty. As fast as he could move with his bad leg, Rudy carried me to the Shotgun. We tore out of the farmyard as though lives were at stake. Many were.

In a mile, we were at the pasture. The scene was chaotic. Impetuously attacking the sheep were eight to ten

---

[13] Hollow-point bullets flatten upon impact to create severe damage when traveling through its target.

dogs—with their random movements they were then difficult to count. And assessing their number was not a priority. Stopping them was.

From the road, Rudy honked the car's horn, he climbed out of the vehicle and yelled at the top of his lungs, and he whistled—or tried to—but the dogs were oblivious to his pleas. Instead, they insanely pursued the frantic sheep, enjoying the frenzy they created. They were mesmerized in the massacre.

Casualties were already evident. Near the fence, not far from the road, lay a lamb, disemboweled and dead. Ten feet farther, another lamb lay dying. Every few seconds he raised his head, bleating for his mother.

Farther away was an old sheep that had been "picked off." Her rear hamstrings were ripped away, and although she positioned her front knees to rise, she had no leverage. Still, out of fear it seemed, she tried, only to flop over with each attempt.

Other victims were evident farther into the pasture, where the vicious assault continued. Rudy had to intervene. He slung me over the hood of the car where he also braced his elbows. The first shot killed a collie-boxer. (I thought collies were bred to protect sheep. Blame the boxer, I guess.)

The second shot slew a spaniel. Later it was determined that this was a prized hunting dog. He, with all his training, should have known better.

The third shot missed. (This was the only time I recall Rudy failing to find his mark. But with the dogs' radical behavior, the distance, and the heat of the moment, I'll give him a break.) Shot number four killed a common mutt, but no doubt someone's best friend. Shot five felled a hound—also a mix, I suspect. Although fallen, it was still alive and in deadly pain. It howled loudly, thereby likely saving its comrades' lives.

Hearing the howls, the remaining mongrels came to their senses, assembled, and sprang for the fence. They jumped over or through, dashed across the road, and charged into a hayfield, out of sight.

Anyone other than Rudy, out of anger or intoxicated by adrenaline, would have blasted them in their retreat. He, however, recognizing a mission accomplished, simply ejected the last spent shell, positioned me in the car, and drove into the pasture to assess the damage.

The old ewe was still languishing in pain. I euthanized her. By the time we reached the once-yelping dog, it was lifeless. Rudy counted six dead lambs and sheep. Several more were wounded. After milking and breakfast, he and the hired man would corral them and apply first aid as best they could.

Driving away, Rudy studied the dead dogs. He recognized at least two. They belonged to families in town. One was unmistakably the pet of a friend. Explaining the events of the morning was going to require delicate communication. It did not go well.

The friend rejected the idea that his dog could ever do such a dastardly deed. And he judged that Rudy killed him out of spite. The accusation hurt Rudy profoundly. He and his friend had joined the Army together. When the war ended, both returned home to find some way to make a living. Rudy turned to farming; the friend operated a local business. One would think that their relationship, built upon common causes, would have been insurmountable, but sentiments for the dog won out, without compromise. From then on, the former friend avoided talking to Rudy, forever.

Other townsfolk whose dogs were implicated also doubted that their faithful pets would gang up for an early morning foray, let alone ruthlessly kill innocent sheep. For them, Rudy had one response: "Come out to my pasture. You'll find your dogs and my dead sheep." It was incontrovertible evidence, though difficult to accept.

I saw the curs in action, so I know. They acted as a mindless pack, driven by deep canine instincts and the thrill of romping freely in the countryside. They were frothy with exhilaration, such that their protective natures, persistent training, and individual self-restraint went "out the window." I understood. So did Rudy.

He forgave the dogs and their owners, while longing for friendships, now lost. Rather than dwell on the half dozen dead sheep, he was thankful for the 494 that still bleated in the pasture, eating their preferred grass to the nub.

Dumb sheep. Ya gotta love 'em.

CHAPTER TEN

INDIAN BATTLE

You have probably wondered how I came to be broken into two parts. I recognize that in my fractured state I hardly look capable of performing as valiantly as my stories suggest. So, I thank you for accepting their truth as well as the circumstances of my demise, which I shall now convey.

I was, in fact, busted in hand-to-hand combat—a fight between two men, both drunk. One, a white man, fired my single shot, missed, and then, hanging onto my barrel, swung at the second, a bona fide full-blooded Indian, who ducked. My stock smashed into a wall and broke off. The story, however, doesn't end there, and I have to go back a way in order for you to understand how it started.

As I mentioned before, the hired man typically stayed for several years, but he eventually moved on. Then, Rudy would find a replacement. That's how Dewey became the hired man. He turned out to be quite a character, particularly when drunk.

Dewey was a free spirit who cared little about material things, except possibly for his car. His clothes were torn and tattered, and his shoes were taped up to hold in his feet— bare feet, I might add, because socks to Dewey were an extravagant accessory. Most noticeable, though, were his eyeglasses, which were alarmingly thick and therefore obviously critical for his sight. What made them most stand out was how crooked and cockeyed they were, plus the haphazard way they were reconstructed with wire. They hung on his swollen red nose, but barely, giving testimony that for Dewey material things took a distant second in importance to alcohol.

But drinking during the day was not a problem. Dewey faithfully showed up at the barn on time each morning, and interestingly, he was typically in high spirits (no pun intended). He energetically engaged in his duties and especially liked working around others so he could brag about his exploits. Most were adventures and grand accomplishments of his past. Who knows? Perhaps some of them were true.

He also liked to brag about his nightlife. He boasted about how many beers he consumed or how frequently he scored with his wife. Although Dewey's manner stopped short of being vulgar, he was clearly proud of his professed extracurricular activity.

Dewey was by nature impetuous. I mean that he was inclined to "do" before "thinking." This characteristic got him into trouble time and again. Once he went sailing off the road into a borrow pit[1] when he let haste supersede safety. Oh, there was a reason for haste, for you see,

---

[1] A borrow pit along a road is its ditch. It is the area from which material was dug to make the road. The excavated area is used for drainage.

another fire had broken out on the farm. But my goodness, you shouldn't have a car accident trying to address a fire. Trading one danger for another is foolhardy.

I suppose to brief you on this account I should start with Tommy's jacket. While shopping for material to sew herself a dress, Mother's eye caught some bright, orange-red-brown material. It occurred to her that this fabric could become an amazing coat for Tommy. She resolved to make him a "coat of many colors" just like Joseph in the Bible had.[2] He could wear it to do mundane farmwork and not look drab in the process. (Although the coat was intended to signify that Tommy was special, it never occurred to her, Tommy, or anyone else that Tommy was set above her other children. To her they were all special.)

Tommy thought the jacket looked hideous, but the care required to sew it led him to wear it proudly. Besides, with its hood and lining, it was warm and comfortable.

Fall days in North Dakota can be hot or cold, even if sunny. On a sunny but cool day, Tommy was wearing the jacket when Rudy spotted smoke rising from a ripening wheat field to the east. It appeared that the wheat was burning. Something seemed to be smoldering, perhaps from a faulty electric fence, though that would be rare. He called for Tommy to join him and together they raced in the Shotgun to the field. By the time they arrived, a breeze, acting as a bellows,[3] had "kicked up" an open blaze. Fortunately,

---

[2] The story of Joseph and his coat is recorded in Genesis 37.

[3] A bellows is a device with an enclosed bag, often made of leather, between two handles. The bag has a small opening opposite the handles, which are spread and contracted to take in and expel air. Bellows are used for building fires, especially in furnaces and fireplaces.

it was on the edge of the field, but unfortunately, it was on the east edge. The fire, buoyed by the westerly wind, would soon be a conflagration consuming the wheat unless it was put out immediately. Rudy and Tommy jumped from the vehicle and began fighting the fire, Rudy with a shovel from the ranch wagon and Tommy with the only means he had—his "coat of many colors." Swatting at the fire to suffocate it, the coat heated up, and soon with each swat a little burned off. His coat was being sacrificed. What else was there to do?

From the farmstead, Dewey saw the smoke and then the Shotgun, and finally Tommy and Rudy fighting the fire. He jumped into his personal car, a green sedan, and sped to the field, without thinking to bring anything with which to fight the fire. When he arrived, Rudy noted his inability and yelled for him to "go back" to the farmstead to call the volunteer fire department.

"Go back" must have registered profoundly for the spontaneous Dewey, because he rammed his car in reverse and proceeded as fast as he could down the same path he had just taken. At the gravel road, he negotiated the turn going backward, instead of stopping to change direction. He was fixated on hurrying. In reverse, he accelerated to nearly thirty-five miles per hour, a green steak preceding a cloud of dust. Then, given the difficulty of steering a car looking at a mirror and the instability of a vehicle guided by wheels now at the rear, the car careened into a ditch, or a borrow pit, as I called it before. The ditch was wet with water at its bottom; the sedan was stuck, and Dewey was out of commission.

I frankly do not recall if the fire department came to the rescue or how the fire was extinguished. The memory of Dewey dramatically flying off the road somehow supplants other recollections. I do know that the wheat field was saved, that Tommy took a long time explaining to Mother that the special coat was expensed for a good cause, and that Dewey required precise communication, especially when he was worked up.

Dewey's wife, Rachel, in her upper 20s or lower 30s, was considerably younger than he. She was a tall, athletic, and attractive Indian woman from the Mandan, Hidatsa, and Arikara Nation.[4] Rachel had a pleasant personality—when she wasn't also drinking—and, quite understandably, grew restless hanging around the house day after day. As a result, and because she wanted extra money, she asked Rudy if he had any work for her.

After several such inquiries, Rudy pointed out that a granary on the farmstead was weathered and if she wanted to tackle that project he would buy paint and pay her for the completed work. She jumped at the offer. So Rudy bought the paint—a barn red color. Oh boy!

Rachel was not a skilled painter. She just knew that the paint had to go from the cans onto the granary and that the sooner she was done the sooner she would get paid. Paint splashed everywhere. Before long the aluminum ladder she was using was mostly barn red. And Rachel? Yep, lots of red—on her clothes, arms, face, and hair.

---

[4] In the mid- to late-1800s, Indians in North Dakota were confined to reservations according to their heritage or identity. They were recognized as a nation.

Everyone admired her determination while being struck by the caricature of a Native American covered in red paint. Images of eighty to a hundred years earlier came to mind—Indians on the warpath.[5] Rachel paid no mind to her appearance, however. She had a project to finish. What's to worry over a little paint?

On occasion, Dewey and Rachel visited the reservation and the home where she grew up. And on occasion, they would return with a family member who stayed with them until they again visited.

Once, they returned with Rachel's younger brother—early 20s, I'd guess. He, like Rachel, was tall and athletic, a handsome young man. One evening the three of them got to drinking, heavily. Around midnight an argument broke out between Dewey and the brother. It intensified and then threats were exchanged.

At the time I was kept in the milk house "at the ready," in case anything untoward required my attention. Dewey knew my whereabouts and when the situation grew hostile, he staggered to the milk house, grabbed me, and, swearing loudly, headed back to his place. Things were not going to go well. Dewey intended to make others see things his way...or else.

The brother made the mistake of calling Dewey a derogatory name. In an instant, Dewey flipped off my safety and fired. The bullet tore into the wall inches from the brother's

---

[5] Indian: the author apologizes if this or other terms of the times and in the story offend someone. He has high respect for Native Americans, their original harmony with nature, their eventual struggles with advancing foreigners, and their current contributions to society.

head. Relieved and recognizing that I was only a single shot, the brother, with bravery bolstered by booze, began cursing Dewey. His mistake! Dewey flipped me around, grabbed me by the barrel, and started swinging. The first swing was wildly awkward and horizontal like a baseball strike. The second was overhand and directed at the brother's head. Mercy, please. He ducked, my stock smashed into the wall containing the chimney flue and the previously fired bullet. The rubber pad on the end of my stock dislodged and went flying off. I broke in two. Dewey cussed violently, swearing to kill Rachel and her brother. While he pulled open the bolt action on the gun barrel and fumbled to insert another round, the siblings ran for their lives...to Rudy's house.

There, everyone was awakened by desperate banging on a door. In a sleepy stupor, Tommy came into the kitchen to see what the ruckus was about. There he found Mother, Rudy, Rachel, and her brother. The latter was swearing and muttering vows of revenge. He declared that he had to have a knife so that he could get that... However, Mother had a declaration of her own: her knives were for the kitchen and that's where they would stay!

Good thing because Dewey was still hot and every five minutes or so he would raise broken me into the air and fire off a shot into the night sky. Sensing his rage, it occurred to me that had I been something other than a single shot, the earlier goings-on would have resulted in a dead Indian—to everyone's shame.

Rachel and her brother were told that they could spend the night in the basement of Rudy's house, where they would be safe. Rudy, always the calculating type, and one who related intuitively to all kinds of people, predicted that if they let Dewey settle down, he'd be fine and would likely forget the whole uprising.

The night grew quiet, but not all slept. Mother, in particular, was too keyed up to sleep. Around three o'clock in the morning, she heard the back door open and someone leave. Where were her knives? No, no one had gone into the kitchen. Nothing to do now, except pray. She did.

Rachel had snuck out. She "made up" to Dewey, and calm returned to the farm. That morning Dewey arrived at the barn happy as a lark and ready for work.

I was tossed into the shop...in pieces.

CHAPTER ELEVEN

Enter Trixie

I invite you to lean back and engage in yet another bull story. If you have had your fill of bull (stories), just skip ahead to my closing chapter. But if you do, you won't know how Tommy was saved from a charging Herman by an otherwise shy border collie. That would be Trixie, who might only have been good for one trick, but she transformed a face-to-face bullfight from tragedy into triumph.

Here's how it all happened. (And how do I know? The galvanized pipe used in the confrontation came from my shop—well, the shop in which I had been tossed like a hunk of junk. But, you know, despite my broken state I observed plenty of goings-on myself, and I heard Rudy, the hired men, and Tommy relate their—dare I say—fortunes and misfortunes. This account is one of both, with the former prevailing, thankfully.)

Dark and early, one morning at 4:45, Tommy once again experienced dreaded trauma. No, no, it was not a dream of

103

a bull bursting through the window, which you may recall formerly had generated fears of the end of life itself. Nor was it the aching pain of another shotgun blast slashing yet another arm. Indeed, in spite of incidents great and small, what Tommy most dreaded was Rudy rousing him by grabbing one of his big toes and then shaking it, plus his leg, and even his entire body, until slumber was forsaken. Actually, after one such experience, any subsequent grappling for a toe awakened Tommy instantly. Call it self-preservation.

Tommy felt Rudy groping for a toehold.

"Hey, Dad! What's up?"

"Had better get dressed. I need you this morning."

"Yeah. For what?"

"I need help closing the gate. Meet me at the corral in ten minutes." With that Rudy limped from the bedroom, through the house, and out the back door.

Tommy swung from his bed and began dressing, thinking, *Close the gate? Why would Dad need help closing the gate? Am I really getting up before sunrise to merely do that?*

By the time Tommy rounded the calf barn to arrive at the corral, darkness was giving way to twilight. Dawn approached and Rudy had herded all but the last few cows into the corral for the morning milking.

By the gatepost stood Herman.

Herman as you certainly know by now was a Brown Swiss bull—remember, the Little Brothers named them all Herman. Like his predecessors, this Herman was both unique and dangerous. Indeed, his uniqueness made him extraordinarily dangerous. Instead of being loud and aggressive like a big bully, he was quiet and cunning. In a word, he was stealthy. He was known to sneak up behind Rudy and the farmhands, and, without bluster or beller, attack his foe, aiming to pin him against some structure, such as a building, or trample him definitively into the terra firma.

Recognizing Herman's tactics, Rudy had outfitted him with a set of blinders and a three-and-one-half-foot chain attached to his nose ring. The blinders prevented Herman from seeing unless he raised his head to peer through slits in the bottoms. With his head held high, he could not effectively charge. If he quickly lowered his head, he faced the very real possibility of stepping on the chain and yanking his nose ring, thereby experiencing excruciating pain. All in all, the blinders and chain were intended to be an impervious deterrent to bad behavior.

But Herman, like I said, was stealthy.

Tommy called out to Rudy, "Okay, I'm here. How can I help?"

"We need to close the gate," said Rudy. "My rheumatism this morning is too much.[1] I can't raise my arms."

Tommy thought, *That's rough.* He had seen Rudy incapacitated before by what Rudy called rheumatism. Maybe it was that, or maybe it was actually some other condition. In any case, he knew that when Rudy was so inflicted he experienced uncommon discomfort, and what little he accomplished would be by force of willpower. But why was closing the gate a particular issue? After all, the chain to

---

[1] Rheumatism is a general term for conditions of pain, including stiffness, affecting joints or tissue around them.

secure the gate was hanging between the corral's boards below Rudy's waistline. He did not need to raise his arms.

Rudy went on, "Sorry, but I can't back up the bull this morning. I need you to do it."

In today's vernacular, Tommy would have said, "Excuse me?" But back then, he simply asked, "Huh?"

Rudy proceeded, "By the calf barn is a long pipe. Grab it. Then smack Herman on the head. He'll take a step back. Once you get him backed up far enough, I'll chain the gate."

Employing an expression of dismay, Tommy cried, "Gallopin' gofers! You want me to walk into the open and beat the bull on the head to move him beyond the gate?"

"You got it. Done it myself many a morning. I'm just too stoved up today.[2] In a few minutes you'll be back in bed, fast asleep."

At that moment, Tommy was clearly and decisively awake.

He could see how the stage was set: Herman, the villain that he was, knew that although he could not sneak up to the man, the man (or boy, in this case) would have to come to him. He awaited his opportunity at the gatepost.

Tommy invoked a philosophical thought: *When in Rome, do as the Romans do. Humph. If Dad did it, I guess I can try.* Thus he complied. Picking up the pipe, he stepped toward Herman. *But wait,* he thought, *why am I risking my life? Didn't Rudy acquire a dog for such daring do?*

That would be Trixie. We were buds, and many were the days when she had lounged in my shop. While nice to have

---

[2] To be stoved up is to be extremely sore or stiff, such that one can hardly move.

a companion, I had to wonder how it was that this border collie was housebound—er, shop bound. Border collies are bred to herd sheep, and they are known to be impressively good with livestock of various types. But not Trixie.

Careful observation revealed that Trixie actually liked being around livestock. She just had anxiety issues! So on that fateful morning, where was Trixie? Answer: cowering (no pun intended) by the calf barn, watching the scene play out—watching!

Worthless cur, thought Tommy as he approached Herman, who waited, head down though twisted to one side, so as to extend the chain away from his feet to avoid stepping on it. Stealthy scoundrel.

Be brave, oh, matador. Get through this, sleep some more, catch the bus, study hard in school, go to college, and NEVER come back to this farm again! These were Tommy's thoughts. *Get through this!*

However, there was another problem.

The pipe was not only long, it was also wide. I mean to say, its inside diameter was about one and three-fourth inches. Moreover, it was thick. Okay, its wall was thick, about one-fourth inch. Translated: the pipe was heavy. Further translated: once Tommy started to swing, the pipe's momentum kept it moving in the arc first initiated, and Tommy could not alter its course. So here's the problem: after Tommy backed up the bull two steps, with two swings and blows to Herman's head, the crafty Herman altered his modus operandi (you know, his method). As the pipe was arcing downward he lunged forward. Instead of landing a jarring crack to the head, the pipe careened off Herman's shoulders. Now vulnerable, two knees were Herman's target. Tommy anticipated contact, smashing pain, and being flipped to the ground. One's brain functions amazingly fast in such occurrences, and Tommy quickly planned to roll swiftly to one side, hoping to avoid the crushing one-ton bovine.[3] The bull would win, but at what cost—knees, life, college?

I want you to know that miracles happen. They might come in unexpected ways, but that does not detract from the thankfulness of the beneficiaries. On this day Tommy would again count his blessings.

In the split second between the pipe smacking Herman on the shoulders and the eventual debilitating collision, Trixie flashed!

Like a rifle's fire, she flashed!

With a blur that no one saw, she somehow sprang from her safe harbor to the point of attack and bit Herman on the top of the nose complete with a growl of authority.

To hear the men talk about it, Trixie's instincts kicked in. They said she proved to be a border collie that day, meant to manage livestock, and her breeding took hold spontaneously. Maybe. Tommy didn't know about that. What he did know was that Herman promptly backed into the corral and Rudy fastened the gate. He also had a new best friend. Yay, Trixie!

---

[3]   The exact weight of the bull was unknown. Bulls vary in weight from 1,300 to 2,600 pounds, depending on breed, genetics, age, and feeding. This Herman was larger than many bulls.

Tommy did study hard, succeeded in college, and never returned to the farm again…except when he wanted to—and he often did. Tommy found out what you have likely surmised (as another saying goes): you can take the boy off the farm, but you can't take the farm out of the boy.

Rudy's farm grew on Tommy. He never desired and never faced another battle with Herman—any Herman. But trials on Rudy's farm formed the fabric that held his future fortunes. Lessons learned, courage mustered, and early morning risings were seeds later harvested ten-, twenty-, a hundredfold.[4] You see, he was bred, raised, and inspired to flash at the right times—like Trixie.

---

[4] Folds are increases. The term is used particularly for grain, which can produce many times more seeds than the one originally planted. A stalk of grain has a head that may have ten to forty seeds, and with ideal conditions, it often grows multiple tillers, each with their own heads of grain.

CHAPTER TWELVE

RETIRED

After I was tossed into the shop in pieces, I was no longer useful and no longer used. Because I was not rebuilt, I would have to say I was gone— at least, in Rudy's mind. Even Tommy jilted me for another rifle. He had become fascinated with a pump-style .22 that had belonged to his grandfather, and that became the tool of choice for my kind of work. I felt slighted and will argue to this day that I was the better firearm...well, if you assess us according to accuracy—after all, I had a longer barrel and a more refined site. But accuracy was not Tommy's sole objective. To him, I was just a single shot. No getting around that.

So in my debilitated state, I was relegated to merely hang out." Maybe you could say I was retired to the shop. At least "being retired" sounds better than unappreciated, discarded, or forgotten. I learned to let it go. Besides, the shop was the center of farm life, and I had an ideal location for continued observation. Moreover, through the years I learned a lot from Rudy, and one lesson was to accept things the way they were. You might say, I could endure abandonment because he had withstood so many more difficulties.

You already know of his physical limitations, his battles with winter, and the trials of raising livestock. And I suspect you have sensed his leadership in managing a farm, hired men, needy pets, and growing boys. I suppose, too, that overall you recognized the strength of a humble yet relentless spirit.

As I lay amidst the odds and ends of the shop, I determined to appropriate Rudy's attitude of resilience, though to be honest I longed for Tommy or one of the Little Brothers to adopt me—glue my stock together, replace my rubber butt pad, screw my trigger guard in place, oil my bolt action, and take a wire brush to the rust. And since I'm being honest, I'll confess that I even dreamed that someone would sand my stock, stain it mahogany, and blue my barrel.[1] Shoot, I had visions of rising like a phoenix[2] from despair to stand tall and shiny in someone's rifle cabinet.

Nope. That wasn't in the cards, as they say. I wasn't rebuilt. I was a goner.

But I accept that. If I was all rebuilt, would you appreciate my stories? Let me ask this differently: Would stories of old times be authentic coming from a rebuilt, new-looking .22? Would my true tales of trials be believable, if I myself

---

[1]   To blue a barrel is to sand away any rust that has developed and then apply a mixture of hydrochloric and nitric acid. This action produces black iron oxide and a blue-black appearance.

[2]   A phoenix is a bird in Greek mythology that rises from its death ashes to new life.

appeared untried, without any scars of use and abuse? I don't think so.

So you see, I give myself to you just as I am. You get the unadulterated me and my unaltered accounts of Rudy's prairie farm. Believe me, I could tell you more, so much more. I have only offered glimpses of the color provided by the hired men. For example, more than one attempted to "hustle" Mother. She would have no part of it and informed Rudy, who responded definitively, as in, "You're fired. Get your things out by nightfall and be gone!"

One hired man fancied a neighbor's daughter, or so he was accused. He was last seen in jail. Another feared snakes. What abuse he suffered when teased with a live reptile! What abuse the teaser suffered when he was subsequently jammed in the buttocks with a three-tine pitchfork.[3] Some ill-fated hired men suffered dreadful accidents. One was ripped apart by machinery that got out of control. Another was hospitalized by a bull, named—you guessed it—Herman. Couldn't the Little Brothers come up with some other name?

Rudy outlasted all the Hermans, teaching them lessons of respect in more ways than bashing them with old cars. But in one case, it was not clear who won. You see, Rudy suffered a heart attack in that bull encounter. He survived but not without permanent damage.

Not only did Rudy suffer damage, so did the property.

---

[3] A three-tine pitchfork is designed for pitching hay. It was particularly popular for pitching hay and straw bundles of yesteryear. Bundles were formed by a binder and stacked in shocks to dry. Later they were pitched unto wagons for transport.

SHOT

There were other fires: the milk house once and the farm-house, too. The well, though a deep one, was contaminated by nitrates, causing calves to be born prematurely. They were weak and susceptible to disease; thus, many died. The sheep fared far worse with most of them aborting their lambs. Without the offspring, the sheep were a losing prop-osition and had to be sold.

Drought came—horrendous drought. To keep the dairy operation "above water," Rudy and his neighbors camped miles and miles away in the Turtle Mountains and made hay from sloughs and meadows. Much of the hay was hauled back to the farm via a grain truck, which Rudy modified with extended racks to increase its capacity.

Drama, however, should not headline most of farm life. No, there was the everyday work, the usual. But what was usual then stands out as remarkable today. Consider spring planting when the usual entailed freeing tractors stuck in mucky soil, or prying from the earth massive rocks that had somehow, over time, risen to the surface. (They had to be removed to avoid damage to the machinery.)

Consider also the usual harvest. When the grain is ripe, time is of the essence. Getting the "crop off" demands long days that often extend into the night, laboring with lighted equipment. Picture swathing in one field and thrashing in another, often with more than one combine,[4] and trucks racing to the combines to receive the grain, sometimes

---

[4]   A combine is technically a combine harvester of grain. Threshing grain involves removing grain kernels from their hulls, which are part of the grain's stalks. In its most complex configuration a combine both cuts and threshes grain. Rudy, however, usually used a swather to cut the grain and form it into rows.

without stopping. (The truck driver positions the truck the right distance from the moving combine and drives forward while the combine augers out its collected grain.) Not a minute is to be wasted.

If you have pictured harvest, you also see trucks lumbering under full loads to bin sites.[5] And you see grain augers, elevated truck beds, and puffs of dust spiraling out from a granary.

Becoming accustomed to the hustle, one scene each day for you would seem peculiar. The combines, normally in a focused rush, have stopped. What gives? Ahhh, Mother has arrived with an afternoon lunch. For this the harvest pauses, and the pause lasts long enough to consume a sandwich and lemonade. And while paused, the men—yes, mostly men, but many women operated combines and trucks, even back then—linger, of course, for a couple of fresh-baked chocolate chip cookies.

Almost as bustling was the annual corn chopping. The chopper in the field pulled a wagon, loading it from silage blowing from a chute. When the wagon was full, the chopper turned out of the corn rows to release it. At that same time, a tractor unhooked an empty wagon alongside the standing corn not far from where the chopper turned aside. When out of the way and stopped, its driver hopped off to hold the empty wagon's tongue,[6] while the chopper

---

[5] A bin site is a location where grain bins, storage units for grain, are established. The more modern bins in the 1950s and 60s were made of corrugated steel.

[6] The tongue is the extension from the front of a wagon that is used to pull it.

reversed to connect and then once again proceed, "throwing" silage into the "new" wagon. The driver then hooked up the full wagon and "flew" to the silage pit where it was dumped. There the Huh-ha (remember the story of the Christmas Ham?) evened out the piles and drove back and forth to pack the silage. It would cure and be fed to the livestock during winter.

With this operation in full swing, Rudy would not permit interruption. Thus, when Tommy came home from school, he was assigned to fetch the cows and see to it that they were properly milked. No silage partying for him.

Now, milking cows was a usual practice. Too usual—twice-a-day, seven-days-a-week, fifty-two weeks a year, every year! It was so routine that it lodged into the subconscious thoughts of Tommy and the Little Brothers. Consequently, in spite of accepting milking as an inevitable chore, they would dream about it. Mother once complained to Rudy that Tommy had been excessively deployed for milking. Her argument: she had heard him in his sleep calling the cows into the milking parlor—"Come, Boss!"[7]

To visitors, especially from town, milking was an impressive operation. Rudy had a three-stanchion parlor. The cows came up a ramp to the parlor to be milked, enticed by ground feed that was sometimes laced with molasses. Umm good—for a cow!

Indeed cows, like most animals, love to eat. They are regular biological factories. And since you're interested in

---

[7]   Milk cows are sometimes summoned with the call of "Come, Boss." Because they are subsequently fed grain after coming, cows become trained to respond to the call.

farm life, you might as well recognize that input generates output, and I don't just mean milk. While in the parlor, cows frequently—shall I say, euphemistically—poop. (Most farmers have far more poignant expressions for this excremental process.) Needless to say, acquiring the milk involved dodging a lot of manure. Beyond appreciating a farmer's plight in negotiating the "friendly fire," you should be intrigued (and relieved) by the care taken to ensure milk is cleanly extracted and hygienically stored.

Yes, yes. I could tell you more, so much more.

From my shop hang out, I witnessed many sights, heard many tall tales, and pondered quite an array of complaints.

So what did I see? Well, I'll give you one: I saw a dog getting his tail chopped off. Okay, technically I did not see that because his tail was already pulled off when the dog was overrun by the Shotgun while chasing cattle. Only the bone remained. The hired man volunteered to get his shotgun and put Rex out of his misery, but Rudy said, "No. We had better shorten things up and let him lick his wounds. He'll heal." He did.

I also saw chickens scalded and de-feathered, machinery invented, and vehicles transformed. And I saw Mother accidentally throw her favorite butcher knife into the shop furnace, where it burned along with household refuse. Later, I heard her swear that knife was stolen by a visiting preacher. Quite an accusation. For months, unbeknownst to him, he suffered verbal harangue and character assault. In the fall, Tommy found the half-burned knife. Mother was chagrined, though not exactly quieted. To her, there was cause for an accusation.

In passing, I might say that some visiting preachers were indeed ripe for reproach. I'll not pursue these stories, but at least one was perverted, others were self-aggrandizing, and some were simply immature. In fairness, many were entirely opposite of all that. They provided wisdom, encouragement, and understandable elaboration on biblical scripture—all of which helped formulate the family's foundational faith.

Back in the 50s and 60s, complaining for many farmers was a recognized sport. (I think that it probably still is.) It was either too hot or too cold; too wet or too dry. Prices were too high—everybody's going to want a piece of the action. Or prices were too low—usually, this was the case, and the farmers vigorously sang this chorus in unison. Well, all except for Rudy. For him, things were what they were.

Tommy once observed a salesman trying to "buddy up" to Rudy by surfacing common complaints. "So, Rudy, how do you like the weather these days?"

"About right, I'd say," Rudy replied.

Trying another tack, the salesman moved on. "Wheat looks like it's going to hold at the current rate. Shameful what that government of ours is doing." (He was a clever dude. He surfaced two common enjoinders in one fell swoop.)

But not for Rudy. "Can't say I think much about that. I'm glad I have a dairy herd to even things out."

"Say, Rudy, how are things going for you? Got enough money?"

Who has enough money? Seems everyone wants more—a clever tactic to solicit complaint to which the salesman could express empathy and gain an edge. But Rudy was undaunted. He replied, "Yep, got enough."

"Be nice to have more, huh?"

"Maybe. Enough is enough." This was an interesting answer because by any local standard Rudy was "dirt poor." But then money wasn't Rudy's measure of worth.

"Fine with that. How's the family? Kids these days can be a real challenge."

"Oh, I'm glad to have 'em. Can't blame kids for acting like kids. Wouldn't trade them for anything."

"Yeah, we all get there somehow, I guess. The wife treating you okay?"

Now, what farmer couldn't complain about his wife, and she about him? It's fundamental to the sport of complaining. Of course, if you live with another person, you know of a number of deficiencies. And Rudy knew some about Mother (and vice versa). He almost took the bait. "Keeps a man on his toes. (He only had five—some expert.) Couldn't live without her. I thank God for her every day."

It was useless. Besides, Mr. Salesman, it was unnecessary. Rudy already saw you as a friend—that's the way he was. In fact, Rudy bought into way too many deals from these visiting "friends." He wasn't duped such that he purchased ridiculous items, but he was known to overpay for them.

Forgive me. I got a little involved in that account. Actually, I'm trying to wrap up.

SHOT

As I was saying, I could tell you more, much more. From my post in the shop, I have had time to reflect on the unusual and the usual. Please savor these glimpses even though I only whetted your appetite for a full course. But frankly, contemplating these goings-on and the stories—true stories, I remind you—that I could relate of Rudy and his farm tires me greatly. As much as I'd like to elaborate and entertain, I confess to having grown weary. I need rest.

You see, I am rusted, worn, and broken.

It's been a long day.

I'm shot.

120

Author's Note

In the course of reading this book, you likely realized that the actual point of view was Tommy's, although all stories are connected to Shot. Moreover, you may have suspected that William Jackson is a pseudonym. It is. But I use it only as a matter of preference, borne of a desire to avoid attention if that should somehow materialize. I have nothing to hide.

The stories are true, according to Tommy's memory and perspective. Another observer, say, one of the Little Brothers, may see things differently—different details, sequences, conversations. But in the main, the accounts, I'm confident, would be similar.

Indeed, I encourage others to share their accounts of Rudy's farm. Each would intrigue. Over the years, when Tommy and the Little Brothers traded stories, they, and others listening, enjoyed each other's unique perspectives. All together, they were compatible and corroborative. At their retelling, sometimes in immediate response to an earlier version, those listening would again smile, chuckle, pine, ache, and cry, as though hearing the story for the first time. Life on the farm was that rich.

I have shared my versions. Let others tell theirs. Thereby, our knowledge and entertainment will be all the more robust.

CPSIA information can be obtained
at www.ICGtesting.com
Printed in the USA
LVHW041257211218
601355LV00004B/9/P